# MAIN STREET DINERS

## Where Hoosiers Start Their Days

BY WENDELL TROGDON

A GUIDE TO 125 OLD-TIME CAFES

Published in the United States

Backroads Press
P.O. Box 651
Mooresville, IN 46158

ISBN 0-9642371-7-2

Cover by Gary Varvel

Maps from Indiana Department of Transportation

Printed by Country Pines Printing
Shoals, Indiana

# CONTENTS

PRELUDE .......... Page 3

## RESTAURANTS BY AREAS

GREATER INDIANAPOLIS .......... Page 11

NORTH BY NORTHEAST .......... Page 35

NORTHEAST BY NORTH .......... Page 67

THE FAR NORTHEAST .......... Page 99

EAST CENTRAL .......... Page 123

DOWN BY THE RIVER .......... Page 143

DUE SOUTH .......... Page 149

SOUTHWEST BY WEST .......... Page 163

# DEDICATION

To the men and women who own and operate restaurants in small towns where folks can sip coffee and jump start their days with homemade food in harmony with friends and neighbors.

# PRELUDE

It is 5:30 a.m. in Pine Village, a western central Indiana farm town. Six men are seated at a round table covered with a worn lace cloth at Keith's Coffee Shop.

One man is dressed in a shirt and tie. His companions are men in work clothes and farmers headed for another harvest day. They nod at the stranger who enters and continue their conversation.

We are at Faye's Northside Cafe in Tipton before daybreak on another day. Customers call each other by names like "Granny" and "Chip."

"Everyone here knows everyone else," explains a pleasant waitress who makes sure we do not leave as strangers.

At the Country Kitchen in Winchester, eggs sizzle on a grill behind the counter, watched over by owner Joyce Caylor. "We (she and her customers) are like a close knit family. When one of us hurts, we all hurt," she tells us.

At the Dinner Bell in Burlington, a group of men sip coffee over breakfast and consider improvements for the town park.

Downstate at The Dutchman in Freelandville, cook-server-manager Virginia Held asks farmers and retirees, "Anyone want more coffee," then explains, "We are nothing fancy. We just try to serve good food and please our customers."

* * *

So much for skeptics who claim our sense of community has been lost, that homemade food is a thing of the past, that neighborliness and compassion have disappeared, taking with them what was once a person's extended family.

"Too little time, too much to do," they lament. Their fears, perhaps realistic in larger cities, would fade among the friendship and harmony at home-owned Main Street cafes that remain in small towns across Indiana.

Our objectives for this book were simple. We wanted to seek out Indiana restaurants that remained at the turn of a millennium much as they were in the mid-1900s. We found them in small towns and cities, crowded at times with customers despite the fast food restaurants that serve scripted food amid an impersonal atmosphere.

We found them on Main Streets throughout Indiana, from Lagrange to Tell City and from Kouts to New Harmony.

And we found most of them continue to cook meals from scratch, the old-fashioned way. Items still are served to order by women—and a few men—who take pride in their skills.

Many diners have changed little. Overhead fans twist under high ceilings, some coated with hammered metal from an earlier time. The aroma of eggs and bacon wafts in waves from grills behind counters.

Each diner is different, the clientele the same. A man's wealth or position is not important. Bankers and lawyers sit with farmers and laborers around "liars'" tables and debate sports, politics and local issues. One man's opinion weighs as much as another.

They sometimes are joined by women, who often, however, prefer their own tables away from the banter of male compatriots.

We intended to—and did to a great extent—limit our stops to restaurants on Main Streets. Some are included that are just off Main Streets or are on main traffic avenues with other names other than Main. We also attempted to visit each of the 125 diners that are mentioned in this book for breakfast. It was later in the day, however when we stopped at a few.

We found many of the Main Street diners on the ground floor of old two, sometimes three-story, buildings. Most were in the centers of what were thriving business districts before the Wal-Marts and the Kmarts came to lure away retail customers.

We omitted fast food chains, the Cracker Barrels, the Denny's, donut shops, specialty and ethnic restaurants and small town taverns, some of which also serve good meals.

Our purpose was to capture the flavor of cafes where men and women gather each morning to start their days with coffee and conversation.

We found Hoosiers eager to greet a new day at 5 a.m., sometimes earlier, surrounded by friends and neighbors at round

tables in cafes they make their homes away from home. All were greeted with a genuine "good morning" or by a server's jocular comment that was returned in kind.

We listened as men recalled stories from a half-century earlier and talked about Farmall H tractors that replaced horses and themselves were outdated by bigger stronger machines.

We heard couples say grace before breakfast, causing others nearby to cease their conversations in respect to them.

We learned that one restaurant's motto applies as well to many others. It's slogan: "Where the sun shines on a cloudy day."

— Wendell and Fabian Trogdon

## OUR TOP 10 LISTS

It is difficult to rate 140 restaurants, but we offer these opinions, which are arbitrary and probably argumentative. The lists are based on our experiences. Readers are free to disagree for, like books and wine, each person has his or her own choices of the diners they prefer.

### BEST TEN OVERALL

Town Square, Howe
Cafe Max, Culver
Country Kitchen, Jasonville
Kathy's, Morgantown
Marty's, Beech Grove
Koffee Kup, Kouts
Clayton Cafe, Clayton
Jackson Street Cafe, Cicero
Cardinal Cafe, Veedersburg
Janet's Kitchen, Rensselaer

### MOST LIKE MID-CENTURY

The Freezer, Tell City
Country Kitchen, Winchester
Kate's Coffee Shop, Portland
Dot's Diner, Jonesboro
Dinner Bell, Salem
Jock's Lunch, Corydon
Cody's Cafe, Fort Branch
Biff's Pioneer House, Mooresville
Corner's Restaurant, Rushville
Velma's, Shoals

### MOST INTERESTING

Farmer's Daughter, Akron
Cafe Max, Culver
Quarry Diner, Stinesville
Gosport Diner, Gosport
Harold's Restaurant, Poseyville
Evergreen Cafe, Rochester
Faye's Cafe, Tipton
Marty's Bluebird Cafe, Laketon
Mom's Restaurant, Lagrange
Locust Street, Boonville

### BEST FOR FAMILIES

Town Square, Howe
Weber's, Rockville
Essen Haus, Converse
Ye Olde Downtown, Waldron
Cardinal Cafe, Bloomfield
Stepler's, Amboy
Don & Dona's, Franklin
Dinner Bell, Burlington
Essen Haus, Odon
Windell's Cafe, Dale

## FRIENDLIEST

### (Servers and customers)

Family Cafe, Knox
Faye's Cafe, Tipton
Farmer's Daughter, Akron
Mona's, Van Buren
Corner Cafe, Nappanee
Kate's Coffee Shop, Portland
Country Kitchen, Winchester
Hap's Restaurant, Linden
Ann's Place, Jasper
Rosie's Cafe, Goodland

## BEST THEMES

### (Collections/decorations)

Koffee Kup, Kouts
Cafe Max, Culver
Locust Street, Boonville
Bluebird, Laketon
Cardinal Cafe, Veedersburg
Uptown Cafe, Orleans
Gosport Diner, Gosport
Bulldog Cafe, Lapel
Harold's, Poseyville
Country Kitchen, Jasonville

## A MAN'S OPINION

Among the Main Street diners that men likely will enjoy more than women are Keith's, Pine Village; Cody's Cafe, Fort Branch; The Chatterbox, Hillsboro; Ye Olde Downtown, Gosport, and The Corner Restaurant, Rushville.

## A WOMAN'S OPINION

Main Street diners women may especially like are The Town Square, Howe; Country Kitchen, Jasonville; Jackson Street, Cicero; Bluebird, Laketon: Kathy's, Morgantown; Morninglory, Beech Grove, and Cafe Max, Culver.

## OTHER OPTIONS

Readers may also find places to eat in other small towns. Some of those places may be at general stores like those in Cutler, Lexington, Williams, Selvin, Abington, Freetown, Judah and other communities. Some may be at eating spots like the Hitchin' Post in Norman.

Most of them welcome strangers as we learned in our research for other books such as *Indiana General Stores/Vanishing Landmarks and Backroads Indiana.*

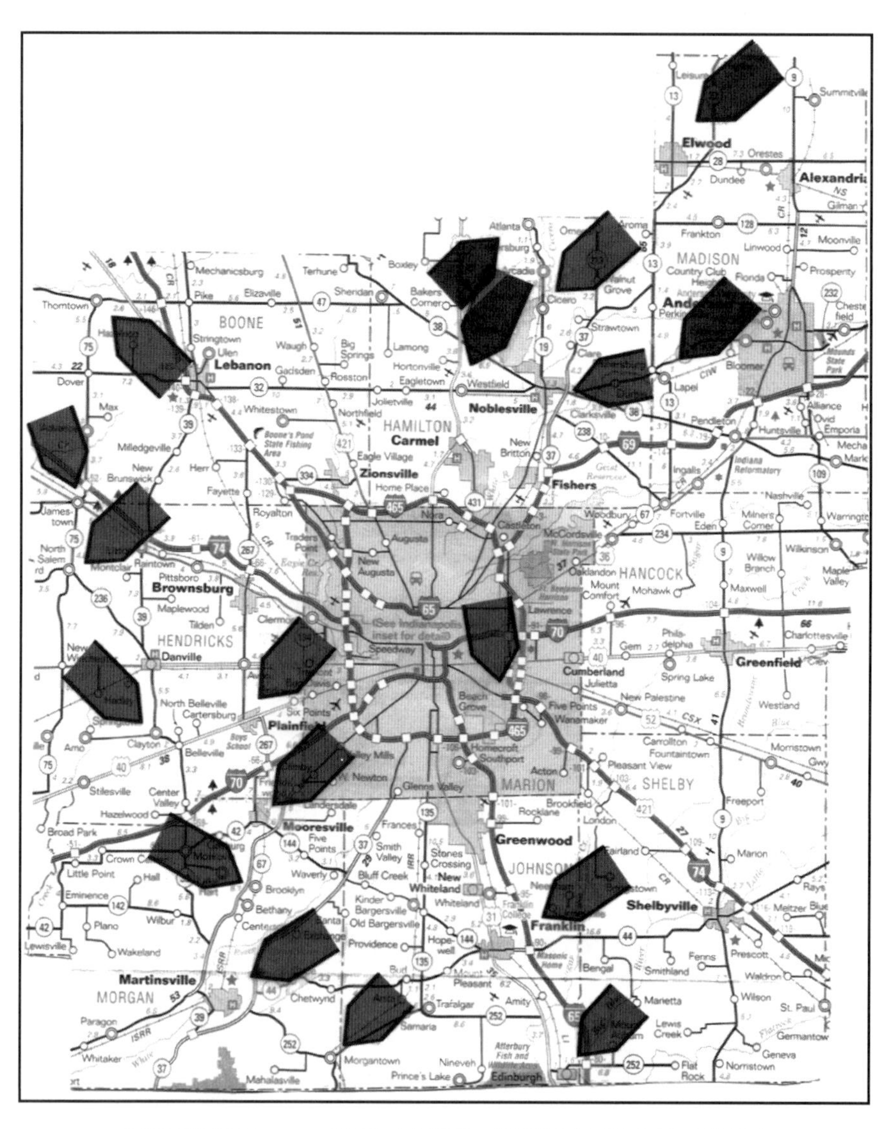


# DINERS — GREATER INDIANAPOLIS

# GREATER INDIANAPOLIS

## BEECH GROVE

### MARTY'S MORNINGLORY CAFE
**607 Main Street**

Surrounded by metropolitan Indianapolis, the city of Beech Grove has retained a small town atmosphere. That sense of community is evident at Marty's Morninglory Cafe on Main Street in the heart of the business district.

A cross section of customers are here for breakfast, among them retirees from factory jobs, young couples, a few children, some businessmen and women. It is a diversity that makes the cafe different from other Main Street diners where a majority of the customers are older men and women.

Outside, the front is brick and frame, the bricks red, the wood yellow. The inside is clean and orderly with tables covered in green cloths. Imitation brick covers the lower section of the walls which are painted at the top. The walls are decorated with pictures, crafts and knickknacks. The floor is carpeted, the ceiling lights recessed.

The menu, enclosed in plastic, promises "the world's finest coffee," which indeed is better than that served at fast food restaurants where the servings are tasteless and the service is impersonal.

A Bible verse is on the menu, the only one we have seen on this tour of Indiana diners. From Proverbs 3:56, it reads, "Trust the Lord with all your heart and lean not unto thine own understanding but acknowledge Him in all thy ways and He will direct thy path."

It's not surprising to see a waitress named Marilyn hug two small boys when they leave for school after breakfast. A customer notes, "It's not everywhere you can get a hug and good food, too." The server confesses, "The hug makes me feel better. I'm doing it for myself."

The oatmeal we find is home cooked and the biscuits and gravy, $2.50, exceptional, for we have become connoisseurs of what has become a favorite Hoosier breakfast.

Breakfast, served from 6 a.m. to 10:30 a.m. Mondays through Fridays, includes a cheese omelet with hash browns and toast, $3.60. Another item rarely offered at Main Street cafes is the cantaloupe.

Among the lunch items are grilled chicken with two vegetables and a roll for $4.65. Available, too, are fish and roast beef at $4.50. For the health conscious, a diet plate also is on the menu.

The carry out business appears big, with someone picking up an order every few minutes.

This restaurant owned by Marty McKenna, is a cut above the average. It's a good place to stop for the soul and the stomach.

## FRANKLIN

### DON & DONA'S RESTAURANT

**18 East Jefferson**
**(Just east of Main Street)**

The menu for Don and Dona's Restaurant in downtown Franklin boasts that it is where good friends come to eat.

It must be. From the size of the crowd at mid-morning on a Saturday it appears to have attracted both friends and strangers. Almost every table is full. The guests, who appear to number at least 100, include teen-agers, young couples with toddlers, professional men and women and retirees.

It's a spacious restaurant that attracts a diverse group, from department heads at Franklin College to graduates of Hard Knocks University.

Few leave the restaurant, which is across the street from the Johnson County Courthouse, disappointed. As with all businesses at the turn of the millennium, it also has a help wanted sign and a notation on each table explaining:

"We are temporarily understaffed. We will serve you as quickly as we can. Our food is homemade and cooked to order. Please be patient and understanding." No one is heard to complain about the delay, which isn't long, anyhow. Orders are filled quickly, and as specified. And you can relax over a cup of coffee without having to wait in line as at a McDonald's or Hardee's.

Don and Dona's is at street level in a three-story building on the northside of the square on Franklin's main east-west street, a half block from Main Street. Inside, the floor is carpeted, except for a section that is covered with hardwood. Tables are covered and huge murals are on the walls.

If any morning visitors leave hungry it is their own fault. The "Country Breakfast" includes two eggs, two strips of bacon, two sausage links, fried potatoes and one biscuit with gravy or toast for $5.25. A 10-ounce T-bone steak with two eggs, fried potatoes and toast is $6.75. Two biscuits with gravy and two eggs are $3.75. Three hotcakes are $2.90. Omelets range from $2.75 to $4.75 for the western or for one called the "Country Gravy."

Lunches are varied. Roast beef, for example, with two vegetables is $5.75, cod fish, country fried steak, fried chicken and some other choices are $5.25. A country fried steak sandwich is $4.25, a double cheeseburger is $3.50. The roast beef Manhattan is $4.95.

The menu notes, "We're proud of our food and service. We're here to please you. We hope you will return soon."

Few will depart disappointed. Most of the customers do return, day after day or week after week, some being known to get in a snit if their seats are taken when they arrive.

## EDINBURGH

### BERTHA'S PLACE

**115 East Main Cross Street**

A sign out front of this cafe in the heart of Edinburgh promises "good home cooking." There is no need to contest the claim once the food is served.

Bertha's Place, its front covered in wood panels, is in a lower section of a two-story brick. From the street it, like many small town diners, does not appear impressive.

It has a different look inside, however. The dining area is almost full at 8:15 a.m. on this Friday morning for this is where many area residents choose to start their days. It is a diverse group, from men bent on conversation with other men to retired couples intent on previewing the day ahead.

As in other small town diners, there is little pretense. A man does not let the bib overalls he wears deter him from conversation with a businessman in shirt and tie. Other men at the table wear hats for Glidden Paints, seed corn companies and assorted other businesses.

The friendly atmosphere is accentuated with cheerful waitresses who, without being asked, make sure coffee cups remain full. Service is prompt, the food is good, the prices reasonable. We order pancakes, a grandson asks for a sweet roll. With coffee and juice the bill is $5.09.

We jot down the hours in case we are again in the area. Breakfast is served from 5 a.m. to 11 a.m. and lunch from 11 until 2 p.m. Mondays through Saturdays. Bertha's Place is not open on Sundays.

## MORGANTOWN

### KATHY'S CAFE

**159 West Washington Street**
**(Washington is Morgantown's main street)**

This is one of Indiana's best known hometown diners, a must stop for most people who are headed south through town to scenic Brown County.

It is open from 7:30 a.m. to 7 p.m. Mondays, Tuesdays, Wednesdays, Fridays and Saturdays. So beware! If you're planning to drive miles for a slice of Kathy's famous butterscotch pie, remember the place is closed on Thursdays and Sundays.

Like most restaurants in the heart of business districts, this one, too, is in an old two-story brick, which a stone inlay indicates was built as a Masonic Hall in 1903. Apartments remain on the second story.

Outside in warm weather, flowers grow in wooden half-barrels out front. Flowers also are in the side windows of an inset for the entrance.

Inside, one side wall is paneled, another plastered. Acoustical tile covers the ceiling; inlaid tile of various colors covers the floor. Pictures, wreaths and others items decorate the walls.

Hardwood booths are on each side of the 20-foot-wide restaurant. Maple tables are in the center. Six stools are at a counter that separates the dining room from the kitchen.

Be it breakfast, lunch or dinner, diners are certain to find a menu with a wide selection.

"Country fresh breakfasts" include, for example, three eggs with ham, sausage patty or bacon and toast and jelly for $4.25. Three hotcakes with two sausages are $4.15. The breakfast special is biscuits and gravy for $2.25.

A bottomless cup of coffee, with breakfast or any meal, is just a dime. Without food it's just 50 cents.

Three lunch/dinner specials, with two vegetables and a salad are available. On Mondays, those specials are the Swiss steak, $6.00, the baked ham, $5.50, the sauerkraut and jumbo wiener, $5.00. The entrees are different each day, with half orders permissible for most options.

Only the strong of will resist the desserts, be it cheesecake or pie, each for $1.50. Most of the pies, like the butterscotch, are unmatched anywhere.

You may have to wait for a table at Kathy's at peak times for this is a popular restaurant, one where the service is good, the "down home cooking" great and the "homemade pies baked daily" good enough to take home.

The place almost makes Brown County a secondary reason for visiting the area.

## BROOKLYN

### THE BRICKYARD CAFE

**6 North Main Street**

From the outside it appears the Brickyard could be named for the bricks that once were made in town. Step inside, however, and you know the name also applies to the Brickyard 400, the NASCAR Race run each August up at the Indianapolis Motor Speedway.

The brick walls in the restaurant in an old building near the Town Hall are lined with NASCAR reminders. A sign at one booth notes it is reserved. For "Dale Earnhardt fans parking only," it reads. A table is for parking only by Jeff Gordon fans. Earnhardt and Gordon, of course, are two of NASCAR's most noted drivers.

A large sign, "Welcome NASCAR Fans" is on one wall. Numerous pictures related to NASCAR are on the walls.

Four four-seat booths are on one wall, four four-seat tables along the other. Two eight-seat tables run down the center.

Three men are at one of the tables, telling fish stories and relating their plans for the day at the 8 o'clock hour. A man enters and is greeted by the server with, "What can I get for you, honey?"

"Honey" orders biscuits and gravy and chooses a table by himself.

A few minutes later, the waitress asks anyone who wants to answer if he or she has seen "Taylor and Lillie." It is obvious the two are regulars at the restaurant. There seems to be some concern about their absence until someone reports assuredly, "Oh, they'll be here, eventually."

In small towns folks care about one another. And this is a place, says owner Kyla Underwood, that caters to a cross section of folks, be they families, farmers, construction workers, retirees or those self-employed or in professions.

She took over what had been known as the Firehouse in 1996, made sure everything was cooked to order and decreed there would be no powder mixes used such as instant potatoes. You order "spuds" or "taters" here and you get the kind that have been peeled on the spot.

Her breakfast special is the $2.50 sausage, egg and cheese sandwich with coffee. We order a single pancake. "Thick or thin?" asks the waitress, bringing reality to the "cooked to order" promise. "How do you normally fix them?" we ask and are told, "However you want them."

We choose "thin." It covers the entire plate and it's good enough to make the Cracker Barrel up at the I-70 and Ind. 267 interchange envious.

Despite the breakfast crowd, lunch brings a majority of the Brickyard's 100-plus daily diners. The lunch special is chicken and noodles, mashed potatoes with gravy and green beans, which is $5.25, about what a sandwich would cost at one of those chain restaurants.

Smoking is allowed, we surmise. The waitress lights up as she relaxes between customers.

The Brickyard is open from 6 a.m. to 2 p.m. Tuesdays through Saturdays. It is closed Sundays and Mondays.

## MOORESVILLE

### BIFF'S PIONEER HOUSE

**14 East Main Street**

Drive by Biff's Pioneer House any morning between 6 and 7 a.m. and you'll see six, seven, maybe eight pickup trucks in a row out front.

The diner has been a popular eating place for six decades or more, a stopping point for men headed for work, a golf course, a fishing lake or back home for another day in retirement. It's a place where men in suits and shined shoes congregate with men in bib overalls and muddy boots.

Sooner or later they learn each other's names and get to know one another well enough to exchange stories and personal problems.

Bill Holmes is one of those men who is at Biff's almost every morning. "It is," he says, "the only place at 5 a.m. where you can get fresh eggs to order, fried the way you want them, not the powdered kind. It also is the only place in Mooresville you can get hot oatmeal."

(Perkins across town serves eggs at diners' requests after 6 a.m., which is too late for men who have to be on jobs at 7 a.m. And its oatmeal is the instant add-water-heat-and-serve kind).

Food, though, is not the only reason that draws men (oh, a few women show up at times) to Biff's. "Another reason," Holmes adds, "is the friendship and the camaraderie that exists among the early morning crowd. It is a place where one person is as good as another, regardless of his station in life."

Holmes, a retired Eli Lilly & Company employee, mentions other regular diners like a man with a doctorate degree, a retired postmaster, two men who design and build airplanes as hobbies, and others who build homes and run businesses. “It is a certain bunch each morning,” he explains.

They all learn, sooner or later, whose comments to believe and whose to take, as Holmes says, “with a grain of salt.” He knows. He has been a regular diner at the Pioneer House since 1972. “I started with a cup of coffee, then it got to be a bowl of cereal.” And later it was those fresh eggs, fried to order.

Food aside, he adds, “If they didn’t sell anything, as long as the doors were open, we would be there to talk.” It is a camaraderie that continues despite the cigarette smoke, which Holmes agrees “is bad.”

Once known as a bakery with a restaurant it now is more of a restaurant with a bakery.

Behind the bakery cases, full in the early hours, are three two-seat booths, served from a counter at the side. Across an aisle are seven four-seat booths, almost always full in the early hours of the day.

The low ceiling is lighted by rows of fluorescent lights. The floor is tile well worn by the footprints of men like Bill Holmes and his morning associates. Aviation-type pictures are on the walls as are reminders of an earlier owner, Charles “Biff” Hornaday.

A dining room off to the side can seat another 50 or so customers. If you stop by on a Saturday morning, you’ll likely find most of those seats occupied.

The Pioneer House is open from 5 a.m. to 2 p.m. Mondays through Saturdays. It is closed on Sundays and most holidays.

## PLAINFIELD

### KRISTY’S CAFE

**404 West Main Street**

This is not a downtown diner from an earlier era. It occupies an entire 20-year old, one-story brick set back from Main Street, which also is U.S. 40, the National Road.

One neon "Kristy's Cafe" sign is at curbside, another on the front of the building. A sign for homemade pies is at the curb of the cafe, which is a block west of downtown Plainfield. All parking is off the street in spaces near the restaurant.

Seating is available at tables—there are no booths—in the smoking and nonsmoking areas. Ten seats, not stools, are at the low counters.

Modern light fixtures hang from the ceiling over carpeted floors. Walls are paneled at the bottom, papered above and separated by a border.

Breakfast, served from 5 a.m. to 11 a.m., features "The Challenge," which includes three eggs, two strips of bacon, a choice of two patties or two sausage links, home fries and a half order of biscuits and gravy.

Three pancakes with a choice of three strips of bacon or two sausages is $3.25. The menu notes that a third egg is always free... "just ask." A full order of biscuits and gravy, two eggs (unless you ask for a third) and home fries is $3.95.

Plainfield is not a one-restaurant town, not with a Hardee's, two McDonald's and numerous other restaurants, so it is not surprising Kristy's is not packed with local diners at 7 a.m. Six men are at a big table in the smoking section, their laughter about the only sound.

Two men are at the counter and another senior citizen is alone at a table in the non-smoking area, his thoughts more on the morning news than conversation.

The crowd is much larger at noon. Most of the tables are filled with workers from assorted occupations. They have come to choose from five entrees, liver and onions, fried chicken, Swiss steak, country fried steak and barbecue riblets. Those meals range from $5.15 for two sides to $6.15 for four sides. The sandwich special is Philly steak with fries for $5.45. The dinner menu features strip or rib-eye steak, each eight ounces, for $8.95. Shrimp is $8.95.

This is a Main Street diner without the colorful cast of characters or the camaraderie of cafes in smaller towns that have retained a more back home flavor.

# CLAYTON

## CLAYTON CAFE

### 76 East Kentucky
### (Ind. 39 - Clayton's main street)

Check this as one of the better small town diners in central Indiana, made that way over the last 15 years by owners Stephen and Betty Hoop.

The cafe is exceptionally clean, especially for its location in a century-old two-story brick built in 1898 by the International Order of Odd Fellows. Two park benches out front face the street, ready for use on warm nights when the crowd is large and there may be a wait for tables.

The food is good, the servers friendly, the surroundings pleasant in the two dining areas. A small grill is behind the counter which faces one wall in the main room. An opposite wall, papered above three feet high paneling, is decorated with pictures, baskets and wreaths.

On the back wall in front of the kitchen are additional plaques and pictures, including one of the 1947 Clayton High School basketball team that won the Hendricks County championship as well as the sectional.

Three combination lights and fans are on the ceiling. Over the front door for all diners to see is a "Welcome Friends" sign. Another dining area is off to the side, allowing the cafe to have both smoking and non-smoking areas.

Menus are padded, attractive and extensive. Place mats advertise area business.

The cafe is open for breakfast, lunch and dinner, the busiest meal varying by the day of the week. No matter the day, however, the cafe can count on a group of farmers being there at mid-morning. They can be found at the "liar's table," discussing, the Hoops tell us, "a range of topics you can only imagine."

When there is a lull in the conversation, they likely savor the biscuits and gravy, which are among the cafe's specialties. Specials for later in the day may include meatloaf, catfish, beef ribs and pan fried chicken.

Friday is a big night in Clayton. That's when catfish is served, $5.95 for whole fish, $6.95 for filets. Specials differ by the night, Tuesday's for example being spaghetti and meat sauce for $6.99.

The restaurant is open from 6 a.m. to 8 p.m. except on Fridays when it remains open until 9 p.m. It is closed on Sundays.

So what makes the Clayton Cafe different from others? The Hoops say it is "the hometown, homey, down to earth atmosphere and a different all you can eat special each weekday evening."

That plus the ability to make customers feel special, even one who starts to walk out without his hat. A server stops him, hands him the hat, point to others left behind by other forgetful customers and says, smilingly, "We don't need another."

"All our customers are very special people. They make our business," Steve and Betty Hoop agree.

## NORTH SALEM

### LIZ'S COUNTRY CAFE

**6 East Pearl Street**

**(Ind. 236 - Town's main street)**

It is obvious from the street that Liz's Country Cafe is not your run-of-the mill small town diner.

The building is brick and well maintained, a reflection of the attention old buildings have been given in this northern Hendricks County town. Drapes cover the floor-to-ceiling windows that front onto Pearl Street. An alcove, inset at the entrance, is decorated with silk flowers.

Inside, the floor is carpeted, the concrete walls painted in light green pastel above five feet high paneling. Pictures decorate the walls.

Liz Freeland, the owner since 1966, is in the kitchen, preparing breakfast orders. A waitress greets us not as strangers, but as new friends.

It is 7 a.m. and five men are seated at a table, their daily meeting place. Some are retired. Others are here for coffee and food to kick-start their day. They all know each other. The talk ranges from the soybean crop, to NASCAR drivers, to sports to the news of the day. Other men enter later. Some join those already present. Some nod greetings and take tables nearby.

They are regulars who need no menu to know a breakfast of two eggs, bacon, ham or sausage is $3.50, or what is the daily lunch special. And they likely are aware that when they return at noon they can order a bacon and ham club sandwich with chips for $3.75.

We choose a half order of biscuits and gravy and are surprised it comes with two biscuits. The serving is excellent, making us wish we had asked for a full order, which probably would have come with three biscuits. Our companion prefers a single pancake. It covers the plate. The two orders, with filled and refilled coffee cups, comes to $4.73.

A sign reads, "Ask about our homemade pies." We will do that when we return for lunch on another day.

Liz's Country Cafe is open from 5:30 to 2 p.m. daily, with breakfast available until 11 a.m.

## JAMESTOWN

### DICK and JUDY'S

**34 East Main Street**

From the street, Dick & Judy's looks like it may be an ordinary Main Street diner tucked into a hole between walls.

An unadorned brick front gives no indication of what's inside. An entry at the corner of the building is lined with business cards, bills of sales and advertisements for fresh eggs, sweet corn and other home-grown garden products.

The look is different inside. The dining room—no more than 20 feet or so wide—has seats at tables for 52 diners. Four stools are at the small counter. Walls are painted above four-feet-high paneling. Lest partisan backers of each be offended, both Indiana University and Purdue University posters are on one wall.

A sprightly male, who appears to be well into his golden years, is waiting tables at 8 a.m. on this morning. His customers are all men except for two women at one table and a man and woman at another. All appear to know each other and feel free to update news of their families and events around town.

The breakfast menu, with a "Thank you for starting the morning with us" greeting, is extensive. "Our Big Breakfast"—two eggs, ham, bacon or sausage, hash browns or home fries, plus a biscuit and gravy is $3.95. So is a breakfast of two eggs, ham, bacon or sausage, and two pancakes. We choose the pancakes without the eggs.

Meantime, the owner is reordering supplies as a salesman types what is needed into a laptop computer.

The two women leave. The waiter laughs, then explains, "They won't get far. They left their keys on the table."

A diner takes the keys in an effort to locate the women. She doesn't need to go far. The two women are just outside the door, still engaged in conversation. It's like that in a small town where friendliness is the No. 1 priority of the day.

## THORNTOWN

### THE LOST FRONTIER

**114 East Main Street**

Right off it is obvious this is not your normal Main Street diner. A western type roof covers the sidewalk in front of the restaurant which appears to occupy what were once three store fronts.

The one-story building sandwiched between two two-story structures is covered at the front with rough lumber painted brown. In the heart of Thorntown's small downtown area, the restaurant is entered through an alcove which gives merchants and professional offices a place to post their business cards and announcements.

Inside, the ceiling is unfinished, the 2 by 8 joists visible as is the duct work. Some walls have been plastered, some have been left undone, the unfinished wood painted. The decor accents the Lost Frontier name. A crosscut saw has a picture painted by an artist. So does a buzz saw.

The menu is not ordinary, either. It is extensive and attractive, an outside picture of the restaurant on the cover. Wreaths and pictures are on display. So are reminders of what was the town's high school basketball teams, the Kewasakees, before consolidation sent students to Western Boone down the road at Dover. The Thorntown team won the 1915 state championship and old glories live forever in a town this size.

It is 7:30 a.m. and the place is busy. Six men are at one table, engaged in conversation over morning coffee served in cups with the outsides coated in advertisements for area businesses. Coffee, by the way, is 67 cents. Most of the booths, too, are filled, including one where four women are as deep in conversation as the men are across the way.

Unlike most Main Street diners there is no counter, no stools.

The breakfast special includes two eggs, fried potatoes, one sausage patty or two slices of bacon and a biscuit or muffin.

The luncheon special is country fried steak, mashed potatoes and gravy, vegetable, cottage cheese or slaw and biscuit, $4.25.

A dining room off to the side, not in use for breakfast, allows for larger crowds for other meals.

Don't hesitate to detour to the Lost Frontier if you're out on Interstate 65 and want a meal that's different than that served at interchanges. Go west on Ind. 47 for six miles to Thorntown and look for the western type building on the south side of Main Street.

## MECHANICSBURG

### SIGLER'S RESTAURANT

**8245 North Ind. 39 (Far Northern Boone County)**

Mechanicsburg is a wide spot in the road, but the restaurant is a place for farmers to gather for breakfast or for lunch at noon. Look for the pickup trucks out in the crushed stone parking area.

## ATLANTA

### MAIN STREET CAFE

**125 East Main Street**

For anyone who wants to start the day in a quiet diner with an attractive atmosphere, the Main Street Cafe in Atlanta is a good choice.

It is another diner in an old building with a brick and limestone front accented with bluish-green wood trim. A green and yellow sign for the cafe hangs over the sidewalk. Small windows covered with lace curtains face the street. Wood benches are out front, available for sale.

Inside, we count 32 seats at booths plus a row of two-seat tables down the center of the dining room. It is neat and clean with the kitchen to the rear.

Tin cans, bottles, trays and other antique items are on shelves high on the walls. Salt and pepper shakers and sugar and sweetener packets are in small wooden holders on bare tables with place mats.

We are here at mid-morning, too late for the coffee drinkers and story tellers, too early for the lunch crowd.

Among the breakfast choices is "The Sampler," aptly name. It includes three eggs, two slices of bacon, one sausage, one pancake and a half-order of biscuits and gravy for $4.75. A bacon and cheese omelet is $3.95.

Lunch, served after 11 a.m., includes ham and beans with hash browns for $4.50, and chicken and noodles, with two sides for $4.50. Among desserts on this day are carrot cake, $2.25, and peach pie, $1.65.

The cafe is open from 6 a.m. to 2 p.m. Mondays through Saturdays and 8 to 2 p.m. on Sundays. Stop in and chances are you won't be disappointed.

## CICERO

### JACKSON STREET CAFE

**40 West Jackson Street**

Call this a cafe that is, literally, a step above the average small town diner. It's necessary to take three steps up to enter the narrow cafe that doesn't appear to be more than 15 feet wide.

The cafe is near the railroad, its "RR" emblem in the sign over the sidewalk at the entrance, which is between the tracks and Ind. 19.

White wood paneling covers the walls, adorned with silk flowers and a few pictures. Small curtains are atop the windows that face onto Jackson Street.

A restaurant has occupied a lower level of the Eureka Building, circa 1896, for more than three decades. It has been operated as the Jackson Street Cafe since 1997 by Alex and Peggy Christopher.

Up to 60 diners can find seats at 13 tables in the narrow diner. Space, however, does not a restaurant make. It's the food and the service and, for both, we find this one is difficult to beat. That's why at least 30 customers still are here for breakfast at 9 a.m.

The group is as varied as the population, the clientele including businessmen, professional men and women, construction workers, factory employees and retirees.

Some are men of the soil who are here for the "Farmer's Special," two slices of French toast, two eggs, two strips of bacon and two sausage links. It is a giant meal for $3.95 that should keep some men on a combine almost until sundown before they are ready to eat again.

Another $3.95 item includes two pancakes, two eggs, two strips of bacon and two sausage links. A cheese omelet is the same price.

We order a one-fourth order of biscuits and gravy, which the owners note is a specialty of the cafe. It is not the small order it might seem. A thick biscuit sliced in half arrives with a heaping coat of thick sausage gravy.

My companion tries the biscuit with butter. "It's the best so far," she says, having already sampled biscuits in 65 Indiana diners. The server appreciates the compliments.

It is not surprising that one of the biggest turnouts of the week is on Saturday mornings when diners who cannot make it on work days come to enjoy the home cooked breakfasts in a leisure atmosphere.

But breakfast isn't the only meal of the day. Jackson Street has menus for lunch and dinner, which attract from 300 to 450 customers on most days.

The lunch special on this Thursday was a beef Manhattan and cup of soup for $3.95, beef stroganoff, soup or salad $4.95 or ham steak, mashed potatoes, one vegetable and soup or salad for $5.25. A cheeseburger was $2.85.

Dinner entrees, which range in price from $5.95 to $6.95, include chopped beef, ham steak, tenderloin (grilled or breaded), chicken, shrimp, catfish fillets, stir fry, chicken parmesan and spaghetti. Each comes with a choice of vegetable and soup or salad.

Menus, attractive and covered in plastic, feature, appropriately, a picture of a locomotive.

The family-managed operation allows the cafe to serve good home cooked food at affordable prices to a diverse clientele from 6 a.m. to 9 p.m. each day, except Sunday.

Customers seem to like the cafe and so do the Christophers. "We've had several restaurants in two states, but Indiana is the greatest," they assert.

# NOBLESVILLE

## UPTOWN CAFE

**809 Conner Street**

**(Ind. 32 and Ind. 38 through town)**

Like most smaller cities in metropolitan Indianapolis, Noblesville has outgrown its small town image. But it hasn't outgrown the Uptown Cafe.

The cafe is in an old two-story building which remains a fixture at the southeast corner of Conner and Eighth Streets across from the Hamilton County Courthouse.

It's a friendly place at mid-morning when many of the four tables and five booths remain occupied. Most of the customers are senior citizens, who find the cafe a temporary home away from home.

A woman at one of the 10 stools facing the grill greets us as we enter, then asks immediately if we watched the I.U. game the previous night. I.U. is, of course Indiana University and she was asking about the Hoosiers' comeback victory over Missouri.

Almost any Hoosier knows the best way to meet another is to talk about basketball. We nod and smile, knowing we no longer are strangers in the Uptown Cafe.

Our five-year-old grandson is with us. He is fascinated by the juke box selector box at our booth. It is not something he has seen at the McDonald's, Hardee's and Burger Kings that lure youngsters with toys and other promotions.

He is impressed when the server brings his pancakes. They are shaped like a bear's face, tiny hotcakes forming the ears, his sausage patty sliced in half to make mouths, the noses and eyes shaped by the butter.

The food here, though, is more than child's play. It is good, the biscuits and gravy tasty, the oatmeal homemade and served in a big bowl heaped high over the edges.

For the famished, the "Big Man Breakfast" includes sirloin strip, two eggs, hash browns and toast and coffee. The most expensive omelet is the deluxe at $3.90. It includes eggs, ham, cheese, green peppers, onion and tomato.

The Uptown is open from 6:15 a.m. to 5 p.m. Luncheon specials on this Wednesday are a chicken dinner, $5.35; a 21-shrimp basket, $5.25, deep fried cod, $4.75. A T-bone steak is $9.95.

The menu suggests diners pause a moment to think about a Bible verse from Job: "Stop and consider God's wonder." Another notation tells diners, "Have a good day and a better tomorrow."

Every small city needs an Uptown Cafe.

## WESTFIELD

### MARLOW'S CAFE

**112 East Main Street**

Marlow's Cafe remains much as it has for 60 years in this increasingly upscale and fast-growing suburban community north of Indianapolis.

"Established 1939," notes the impressive breakfast and lunch menu, its cover a drawing of the front of the two-story white frame building.

It is about 10 a.m. and some customers are here to enjoy the breakfasts that a sign has promised are served any time during the open hours.

This is not your all-day, seven-day-a-week diner. The hours are 7 a.m. to 1:30 p.m. weekdays and 7 to noon on Saturdays, but the shorter days offer diners a diversion from the fast food restaurants that are open out on U.S. 31.

The dining room is small, no more than 20 feet wide, the ceiling with two overhead fans is low. The place appears to be newly-renovated and redecorated, giving it a neat and clean appearance. About 35 seats are available at tables. There are no stools or counters.

It does not appear to be a gathering place for farmers and men who work at outdoor jobs. It seems to be more suited for business and professional types, but that is a personal observation.

A full breakfast menu is available for whatever the occupation. The special is two eggs, a choice of bacon, sausage patties, smoked sausage or ham, home fried potatoes, toast and juice for $4.75. Another option is two biscuits and homemade sausage gravy with potatoes, $4.25.

Anyone who wants a meal that will last until dinner can order the half-pound of chopped steak, two eggs, potatoes, toast and juice for $5.95.

Daily lunch specials are available as is an assortment of sandwiches, such as a hot ham and cheese, $4.25, or breaded tenderloin sandwich, $4.95, with fries, $5.95. As in all restaurants, prices are subject to change.

Our waitress fills our coffee cups, with advertising on the outside, and sits down to her own breakfast, as if further proof is needed that the food here is good.

We note another sign: “Bob’s homemade chili.” If we’re ever through town at noon on a colder day, we’ll stop for it.

## LAPEL

### BULLDOG CORNER

**701 Main Street**

If you aren’t sure why this place is called Bulldog Corner, step inside the corner door under the black and gold awning on the two-story brick.

Dozens of pictures of Lapel High School athletic teams, mostly the basketball squads, that hang on the walls are obvious clues. The teams, of course, are the Bulldogs, the wearers of black and gold who have brought recognition to the western Madison County community for nine decades.

Despite school consolidations Lapel has kept its high school, and its 300-plus students, which still give the town a sense of unity that communities without schools no longer have.

Team pictures date back to at least the 1916-17 season, highlighted by the 1940 squad that went all the way to the state finals before bowing, 38-36, in the afternoon game to eventual champion Hammond Tech.

A small stuffed bulldog rests on the hat tree near the front of the small diner. A giant bulldog is on a back wall. Team pictures line one wall. Group pictures of class reunions are on another wall. Off to the side are street signs like "Purdue Boilermaker Avenue," "Notre Dame Avenue," "Larry Bird Court" and "I.U. Hoosier Avenue."

The dining room, about 20 feet wide, has 20 seats at booths, 18 at tables. The floor is carpeted, the tables bare, except for the place mats. We arrive at "The Corner" at 6:15 a.m. and a number of the regular customers already are there; probably some since it opened at 5:30.

Five men and one woman are at the round table, talking about today, not yesterday. The conversation ranges from the corn harvest to vandalism to leniency of judges to insurance rip offs. A television in the corner is tuned to CNN, but no one pays attention. Local news comes first in a small community.

The Bulldog Corner menu has, naturally, a picture of a bulldog. The breakfast special is two eggs, choice of meat, choice of potato, toast and coffee for $3.95. A full order of biscuits and gravy is $2.75, two eggs with ham and toast is $3.00. Omelets range from $2.50 to $4.15.

Breakfast is served until 10:30 a.m. when lunches, with specials that change daily, are served. Sandwich prices vary from $2.50 for a hamburger to $4.15 for a turkey club.

Jeff and Melissa Bartel, who became owners of the cafe in 1999, say a restaurant has been at the location "off and on" for a half century. It is, they say, the "sit down" atmosphere that allows farmers, factory workers and business people time to see and talk to friends without being rushed. The good food is another reason.

Open from 5:30 a.m. to 3 p.m. except on Sundays, it, like the high school, is part of the glue that seals a sense of community.

As we depart we note a Lapel Bulldog license plate above the door, a final reminder of why the cafe is known as Bulldog Corner. Good food aside, this is a restaurant for any basketball fan or any native of a small town to enjoy.

## ELWOOD

### VILLAGE CAFE

**1424 Main Street**

We choose to stop at the Village Cafe, which is nearer downtown Elwood than Granny's, out at 1912 Main Street.

Unlike Granny's, which is in a stand-alone building, the Village Cafe occupies the lower level of an ancient two-story building whose bricks have been painted a brighter red. The restaurant front is covered with lumber painted red. Rustic caricatures are outlined on the upper level.

This is not one of your fancier small town diners. It is difficult to maintain splendor in a restaurant that is open around the clock except on Sundays when it is closed for the day.

The place is narrow, but long. There are seats for 40 diners plus eight stools at a counter. The grill is in view.

Order breakfast anytime and you'll likely get it. On the menu is the "Hungry Man's Breakfast," which for $4.25 includes two eggs with ham or sausage, hash browns or home fries, a half order of biscuits and gravy and toast. A cheese omelet is $3.85, a western or Spanish omelet, $4.60.

This is a restaurant that appears to have survived for decades and likely will for years to come. It's a long way from the

McDonald's, Hardee's and Burger Kings of today and it is far from upscale. If you want to make an impression on a first date, better take her somewhere else.

The Village Cafe is a convenient stop for anyone who wants a cup of coffee or food any hour of the day. It is not a place to influence a companion.

## WALDRON

### YESTERDAY'S FAMILY CAFE

**101 Washington Street**
**Main and Washington Streets**

We don't expect to find a diner this spacious in a small town like Waldron a couple of miles off Interstate 74 in southern Shelby County. But here it is at the corner of Main and Washington.

Yesterday's Family Cafe occupies the entire first floor of an old two-story brick. The restaurant front appears to be newly painted in pale yellow. The lower parts of the big front windows are covered with white curtains, making an inviting appearance.

A sign onto the street announces today's special: meatloaf or chicken dinner, $5.95 drinks included.

We step through the doors and into the past. It is "yesterday," as the name promises. Pictures from earlier years are on each wall. A half of one side is covered with Lucille Ball memorabilia. Words to songs, favorites for generations, "Take Me Out to the Ball Game," for example, are on the walls. So are pictures of personalities of an earlier era. Scenes from movies are on display, reminders of a time when motion pictures did not have to be rated R or X to attract audiences.

We are not surprised to find a poster of Miss Ball in the men's restroom, which is neat enough to make her proud.

A big checker board covers a table top for two players. Triangle toys, the kind with golf tees in holes are at each table, proving Cracker Barrel does not have a monopoly on the game.

It is obvious owners Rick and Dema McPherson have put a lot of thought into the appearance of the dining area, as well as into the menu. The dining room is as clean and attractive as any we have visited.

Country music is drifting from the kitchen. The dining room is larger than that in most small town restaurants, being 30 feet or more wide with room for 60 customers in uncrowded comfort. The thirteen tables are covered in oil cloths.

It is mid-morning. We are too early for today's special, too late to join the morning gathering. Our server says we should have been here earlier, nodding toward a long table with twelve seats. "It was full an hour or so ago," she says of the locals who congregate each morning to kick off their days by reviewing the news and commenting on everything from prospects for Waldron High School's basketball season to the farm economy.

Business will resume about 11 a.m., she says... about the time the meatloaf and chicken specials are ready to be served.

Breakfast is served starting at 7 a.m. weekdays and 8 a.m. on Saturdays, the menu featuring biscuits and gravy for $1.89, hash browns and gravy $1.89, two eggs with sausage or bacon, $2.95, French toast or pancakes for $2.25, and omelets for $2.80 to $3.95.

Daily specials are available for lunch, which attracts the most customers. Sandwiches include the "Buss Buster Burger" or "Pat's Patty Melt," each of which are $3.75.

Dinners, served Tuesdays through Saturdays, feature steak and chicken, the entrees varying from a ten-ounce New York strip steak for $11.95, to the Hawaiian chicken for $7.95. Dinner comes with a choice of potato, salad and dinner roll.

Hours are limited on Sunday to 11 a.m. to 2 p.m.

The McPhersons say it is the home cooked meals, which are specialties of the restaurant, that attract up to 200 farmers, businessmen and family members daily. The decor, the pictures and the illustrations also are worth a stop for anyone who wants a diversion from the monotony of travel on I-74.

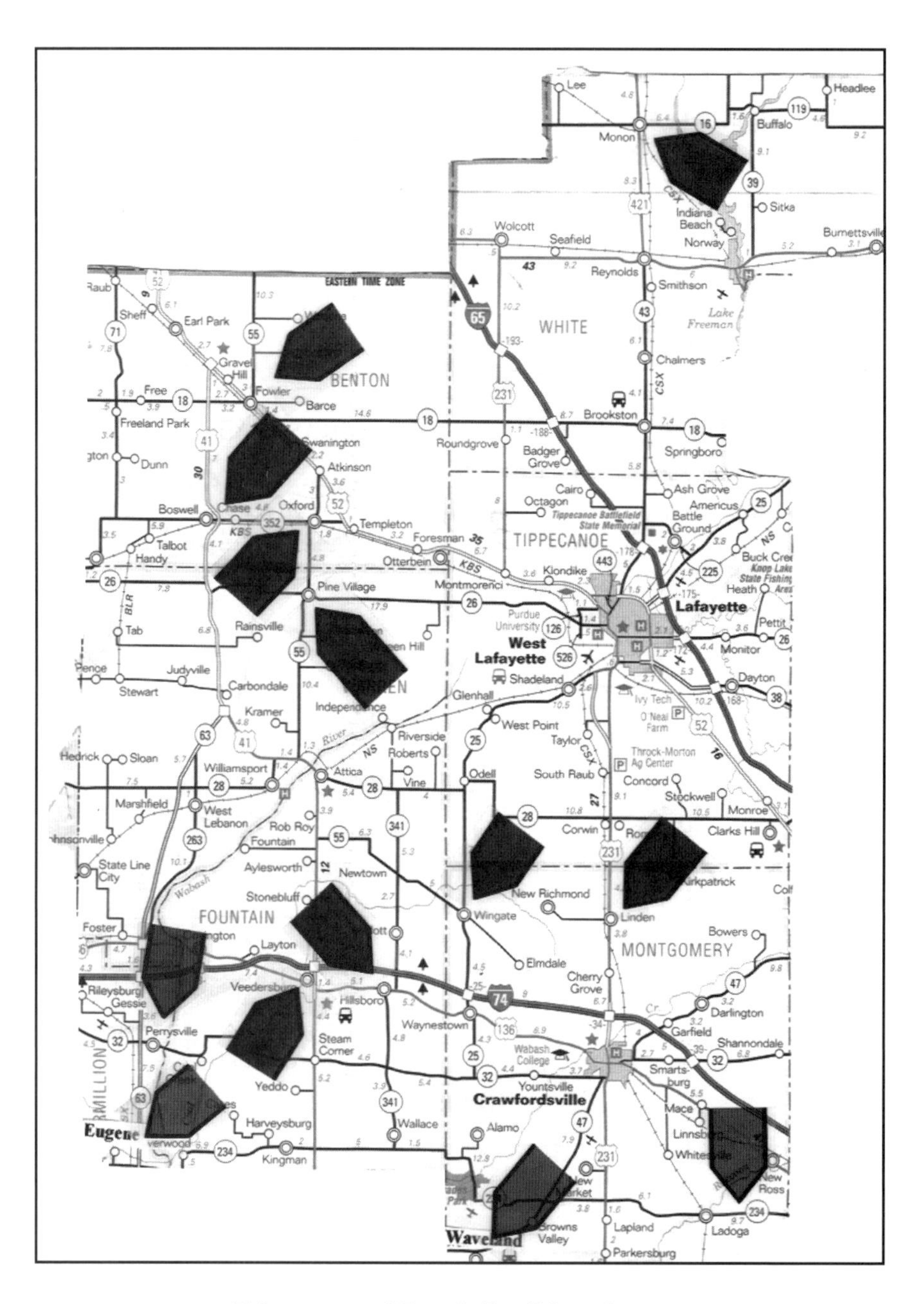


# Diners — North by Northeast

# NORTH BY NORTHEAST

## LADOGA

### THE SUN-UP CAFE
**104 East Main Street**

It doesn't take long to realize this is a cheerful place for Ladoga area residents to come each morning to wake up in sunny surroundings.

Paintings of the rising sun are on both windows near a printed invitation to "Patsy's Sun-Up Cafe—Where the Sun Shines Even on a Cloudy Day."

A smiling face is on the door into the diner which is in the street level of an old two-story brick next to the Centennial Block Building in the heart of what is left of Ladoga's business area.

It is just after 6 a.m. and a number of men already are seated at a long table with sixteen chairs. Another man enters, walks behind the counter, pours himself a cup of coffee, tells the cook what he wants for breakfast and joins them.

Some of the others make their own trips to refill their cups. It is good that they do. The cook/server is alone and the self-service saves her steps. When time permits she talks with the customers about the health of local residents and informs them of any news they may have missed.

It is obvious Patsy's Sun-Up Cafe is a community center for the Montgomery County town. Announcement of new babies are posted on a bulletin board, which includes the names of the parents and grandparents along with the infant's vital statistics.

Dozens of other snapshots are on two other displays in the paneled dining room with acoustical tile ceiling. Booths are on one side of the six-seat table that runs down the center. Tables are on the opposite side. The floor is carpeted.

Pictures of youngsters are on the slick menu, which features a full breakfast and lunch selection. A new breakfast item is the six-ounce rib-eye steak with two eggs, fried potatoes and toast or biscuit and gravy for $5.50. A country fried steak with two eggs, toast or biscuit and gravy also is $5.50.

The Sun-Up opens at 5:30 a.m. except on Sundays. It remains open until 2 p.m. Mondays through Fridays, closing at 1 p.m. Saturdays. Lunch is served after 11 a.m.

If there are dark days in Ladoga, it's not because of Patsy's place. The sun will be shining there, in the painting on the window and in the moods of the earlier risers who come to start their days.

## WAVELAND

### THE UPTOWN CAFE

**205 Cross Street (Main street in town)**

If pickup trucks line the curb of a small town street at daybreak, you know a restaurant is near.

In Waveland, it's the Uptown Cafe owned by Amy J. Isenberg. Hers is not a diner in an old building. It's newer, one story, larger than most. A maroon awning stretches across the front, which is lined with pots of flowers, each abloom despite an autumn chill.

Five tables are occupied at 7:30 a.m. with both men and women customers. Like all small towns, everyone knows everyone else. A man alone at a table asks, "You gonna sit with me, Mitchell?" Mitchell, who has just come in out of the bright sun, spots his greeter and joins him. A waitress serves him coffee without being asked. He is a daily customer, who joins his friend in an endless conversation.

"We want this to be a friendly, relaxing restaurant," explains Mrs. Isenberg, who has been the owner since 1997. It's a family restaurant, one where everyone in the family, including her two-year-old (in 1999) son, Hunter, helps.

This is more than a place for the locals to congregate for breakfast. It's a place for three meals a day, seven days a week, the hours 6 a.m. to 8 p.m. Mondays through Thursdays, 6 a.m. to 10 p.m. Fridays and Saturdays and 6 a.m. to 2 p.m. Sundays.

The usual breakfast items are available, the entree prices including coffee. Two eggs, potatoes, bacon, sausage or ham and toast (and the coffee) are $3.75. A western omelet with potatoes and toast is $4.40, the ham and cheese omelet with the potatoes and toast is $4.30.

The luncheon menu includes sandwiches and sandwich baskets, the baskets ranging up to $6.25 for a double bacon cheeseburger with French fries, slaw and drink. Salads and soups also are available.

The dinner specials, available after 4 p.m. weekdays and 5 p.m. on weekends, change daily. Prime rib and T-bone steaks on Saturdays are $10.95, which includes a choice of potato, vegetable, soup and salad bar, bread and drink.

A children's menu features $3.99 attractions such as dinosaur nuggets.

This is a large restaurant for a small town, one that can seat up to 100 diners in its two dining areas. Its customers include farmers, construction workers, retirees, travelers, campers and other visitors to the nearby Shades and Turkey Run State Parks.

And it is a place to pick up a pizza, with, the menu notes, "lite and crunchy crust."

## LINDEN

### HAP'S RESTAURANT
### ALSO KNOWN AS R & S CAFE

**109 North Main (U.S. 231)**

Memo to anyone who isn't impressed at first glance with the diner at the Hap's sign over the sidewalk in the town of Linden:

Outward appearances can be deceiving.

Sure the two-story brick building is old, a front window glass may be cracked and the place doesn't look as if it belongs on fashion row. But all those things are misleading.

Actually, it no longer is Hap's, despite the sign. It is the R & S Cafe. Has been since about 1995. Owner Sue Hill explains. "My dad was Hap. He bought this restaurant for me about fifteen years ago. When he died, the name was too much of a reminder, too much of a hurt knowing he was gone."

The dining room doesn't look old. The tables are almost new as are the chairs, which can seat 60 or so customers.

Shelves near the ceiling on each side wall are filled with assorted tin cans for everything from potato chips to coffee. Many are collector items from an earlier time.

Walls are painted above three-feet high paneling except for a section near the front that is papered. Purdue University pictures, pennants and posters are on the walls, Linden being just a few dozen long football passes or basketball bounces south of West Lafayette.

Pictures of new babies born into area families are over opening from the kitchen where food is picked up by servers.

On this fall morning, six men are seated at a table for 10 back near the kitchen. They appear to be breakfast regulars. A coffee pot is on their table, saving a server from repeated trips with refills.

If it is the "gossip" table it isn't in use. There is little conversation. Sometimes few words are needed among friends. One of the men looks like Wilfred Brimley. Two are in bib overalls, befitting the rich farm area that surrounds the town.

Sue is the only cook and almost everything served, from the opening at 5:30 a.m. until the closing at 7 p.m., is made by her.

Among the breakfast entries are homemade biscuits and gravy with coffee for $1.95; a half order with coffee $1.55. French toast is $2.25 as are three hot cakes. Omelets range from $2.60 to $4.05.

Sandwich prices are reasonable, a large breaded or grilled tenderloin just $2.25. Friday dinner specials are $8.95 for catfish or T-bone or rib-eye steak. Spaghetti with garlic bread is $4.25. The meals come with a choice of two sides.

This is not a place for pretense or high fashion. It is, however, a place to relax in a pleasant atmosphere and appreciate people like Sue Hill who like what they do and appreciate their customers.

## WINGATE

### THE SPARTAN INN

**101 East High Street Northeast Corner - Main and High**

Big accomplishments in small towns are never forgotten. That's why this restaurant in the heart of Wingate is called the Spartan Inn.

The Spartans were the town's high school basketball teams, including the two squads that won back-to-back state championships in 1913 and 1914.

On display in the restaurant are pictures of Wingate teams of that era. Among the basketball memorabilia on display is a picture of the old high school gym that drew fans to the sport in its infancy.

At Wingate's main intersection, the Spartan Inn is in a concrete block building, with two rooms, the main dining area having seats for 60 customers. Floors are carpeted, the walls painted with a decorative horizontal stripe. The rooms are bright and cheerful.

Two old display cases, the kind found in general stores in earlier years, are in the front room. One contains pies, the other ceramics of interest to collectors. Try a piece of one of the pies. You'll like it if it's as good as the one we had.

If you are a basketball fan or a history buff, stop at the Spartan Inn when passing through town on Ind. 25. The Inn is open from 5 a.m. to 7 p.m. Mondays through Thursdays and 5 a.m. to 8 p.m. Fridays and Saturdays.

## HILLSBORO

### THE CHATTERBOX

**115 Main Street**

The Chatterbox is a Mom and Pop operation. Well, actually, "Mom," is in charge, although "Pop," she says, "is always around somewhere ready to help when I'm the busiest. But I do most of the work."

"Mom" is Dorothy Summers. "Pop" is Melvin Summers, better known as "Pete." The hours for them are long, from 5 a.m. to 4 p.m. Mondays through Saturdays, a total of 66 hours a week. It has been that way since Dorothy decided to buy the place back about 1991.

Their only help comes when daughter Tracy, who works elsewhere, arrives to help out on Saturdays.

"It's a lot of work," Mrs. Summers admits, "but I enjoy cooking for people. I make everything from scratch, except French fries."

The name Chatterbox fits, she agrees. "When the farmers and towns people are in here you've never heard so much chatter." Or as many jokesters, all of whom she appreciates even when some of them attempt to vex her with friendly torment. "You never know what they will come up with next," she adds.

It is just after noon and a half dozen men are seated at a big table near the entrance to the kitchen. They appear to be a cross section of the area's population. One man is wearing a tie, a couple are in overalls, three keep their hats on while dining. They all know each other and the conversation is continuous, but not loud. A police scanner is on, keeping "Pete" and the others aware of what is happening in Fountain County.

But this is not a peak period. The size of the crowd varies. Sometimes, "Mom," is busiest at breakfast, which is served from 5 to 10 a.m. On other days, the peak rush comes at noon. The slow seasons are in the spring when farmers are planting crops and in the fall when they are harvesting them. Those are days when their wives sometimes stop in at the Chatterbox to pick up orders to deliver to their husbands in the fields.

The breakfast menu stays about the same. The daily luncheon special, however, varies from meatloaf to fish. On this day it is chicken noodles, mashed potatoes and cottage cheese for $4.00. Ham, eggs and toast at $3.70 are among the items on the breakfast menu.

The Chatterbox is in an old building in what was once a Hillsboro business block. As in most small towns, stores closed as discount centers opened elsewhere, luring local residents to bigger towns. The building had been used as a coffee shop, a sundries store and a tavern.

The dining area is 20 feet wide, but deep enough to leave room for more tables if needed. The walls are paneled from the carpet to the acoustical tile ceiling.

Extra room allows the Summers to display old Hillsboro and Fountain Central High School yearbooks in racks along one wall. Hillsboro had its own high school before becoming a part of the Fountain County consolidation in 1964.

The yearbooks, the town history "Pete" has compiled and the old *Hillsboro Times* news pages dating back to 1932 add a museum flavor to the business.

The Chatterbox also is a miniature general store and community center. On sale are snack food, candy bars, light bulbs, headache relief, batteries and toiletries, items that customers might otherwise have to leave town to buy.

A bulletin board keeps diners alert to ice cream socials, Town Council actions, auctions and other news. Business cards cover another board.

If you like to dine in down home comfort, the Chatterbox is for you. If you prefer a more formal elegance, this may not be your stopping point. No matter, the Summers like the place as it is. And so do those loyal customers who show up daily to vex Mom and to savor the meals she fixes for them.

## VEEDERSBURG

### THE CARDINAL CAFE

**201 North Main Street**

There is a good reason folks here in Veedersburg call this restaurant on the corner of Second and Main "the new Cardinal Cafe."

The space it occupies in an old two-story brick had been vacant for two years when it reopened in 1998 after a total remodeling gave it a new look.

Oh, it is still entered through a door at the corner, the rest of the building remains much the same, but the restaurant is far different. A new owner, Roy Straw, saw to that, a waitress says.

The new look resulted is an attractive dining area with wallpaper over the three-feet high paneling on the decorated walls. Framed recipes and other pictures are on display. Swinging doors open to the kitchen. The floor is carpeted and tables are covered in oil cloth.

A display case contains a Veedersburg letter sweater. Nearby is a Veedersburg yearbook, a reminder of the high school that was in town before students were sent in 1965 to consolidated Fountain Central.

The restaurant is neat and clean, the lunch menu more extensive than expensive.

Breakfast is not the biggest meal as it is in some small town diners, although the place is crowded at times on weekend mornings. Lunches are busier, especially when pan-fried chicken is served. A diner at another table, interrupts the waitress to say, "And that fried chicken is excellent."

The breakfast menu includes an omelet called "All The Way, " which is $4.75. Pancakes, waffles, and French toast with bananas are other features.

Burger platters, available at lunch, range from $3.15 to $4.00.

The food is good, the surroundings comfortable. The Cardinal is a place to bring guests for breakfast or lunch and enjoy a quiet meal without being upset when the check arrives.

It's open from 6 a.m. to 2 p.m. each day, including Saturdays and Sundays. It's a good place to stop when you are out on I-74 or passing through the area on U.S. 41.

### THE DINNER BELL
**122 North Main**

The Dinner Bell isn't as bright and new as the Cardinal Cafe and it's open only from 11 a.m. to 1 p.m. Mondays through Saturdays, but it is a quick stop for anyone who needs a sandwich.

Mr. and Mrs. Charles A. Boggs II, the owners, carry a different line of sandwiches than other restaurants. "Low-fat hamburgers are cooked on George Foreman commercial cookers," they note.

The Dinner Bell Lunch Counter is a stop-and-go restaurant that caters to 50 or more diners at noon each day.

## EUGENE

### COVERED BRIDGE RESTAURANT
**5787 North Main**

The Covered Bridge Restaurant has a Cayuga address, but it is up the road outside Eugene near its namesake, the 125-year-old covered span over the Big Vermillion River.

The restaurant occupies a rustic building with a number of dining sections, each tastefully decorated by owners Gregg and

Kristy Baxter. Pictures of the bridge can be seen in display cases. Also in view are pictures of old homes and historic places around the area.

A wall of one section is covered with old license plates.

This is not your small town diner where the locals gather for coffee each morning. It is, however, open for breakfast for anyone who wants to wait past sunrise to jump start his days. The menus for all meals are extensive.

Hours are from 9 a.m. to 8 p.m. Mondays through Thursdays. The restaurant opens at 8 a.m. on Saturdays and Sundays when it closes at 9 p.m.

To find the Covered Bridge Restaurant look for the sign on Ind. 63 that points the way.

## PERRYSVILLE

Okay, we're here at 113 South Jackson, the main street in the Vermillion County town of Perrysville. A sign claims we have arrived at the "Perrysville World Famous Cafe."

There's just one hitch. The place is closed. Has been for two years, even though the Internet yellow pages directory indicates it is still in business.

The owner doesn't seem to be eager to sell it, we are told. So be it. All is not lost. Donna's Snack Bar next door is open and busy at sunrise.

### DONNA'S SNACK BAR
**115 South Jackson Street**

Take one step into Donna's Snack Bar and you know this is a morning stop for farmers. Six to eight men are still here, sipping coffee, talking about whatever comes to mind.

Owner Donna McIntosh says it's this way every morning. "The topics may vary from farming to fishing to hunting to the weather, but the customers remain the same. The only change is if someone dies," she adds.

They can order the usual breakfast items, eggs, bacon, sausage, French toast, hot cakes, sometimes both cooked and served by Donna, this being a small operation.

"Breakfast," she explains, "is our main meal. We serve sandwiches later, but except for fried chicken we don't serve full meals."

Five tables are in the small front dining room which has carpet on the floor. A few other tables are in a room to the back. Some antiques are on display, including an old hand-cranked telephone.

Donna has been a fixture at the restaurant for ten years, six as an employee, four as the owner. She has heard the farmers spin the same stories time after time, but there are enough new ones to make the mornings interesting.

After all it remains open while the "world famous cafe" next door stays closed.

## PINE VILLAGE

### ELLA'S TOWNHOUSE CAFE

**Lafayette Street**

It is 6:20 a.m. and Ella's Townhouse Cafe in Pine Village is not open despite a sign in the window that says its hours are 5:30 a.m. to 5 p.m. Monday through Saturday.

"Closed," reads another sign, with no explanation. We learn later it was closed only for the day.

The Townhouse Cafe is in a two-story brick on Ind. 26, which is Lafayette Street, the town's main thoroughfare.

We have been up since 4:30 a.m. and we had hoped to have our wake-up caffeine.

### KEITH'S COFFEE SHOP

**Ind. 55 in Pine Village**

All is not lost, though. We make a right turn to the north on Ind. 26 at its intersection with Ind. 55, and spot Keith's Coffee Shop.

It's in a frame building with a false front, giving an indication of a second floor which does not exist. No matter! We are in search of coffee, not sophistication in dining.

From the outside, Keith's looks like a man's place. It appears even more so inside.

The nearby Townhouse Cafe is closed, but the men here don't seem to mind. At a round table covered with a worn lace cloth are six men, one with a white shirt and tie, others in work clothes, farmers ready for another day of harvest on nearby farms.

They nod at the stranger who enters, then resume their conversation.

The morning news is on the TV but it is ignored, the men more interested in the weather than what is going on in Washington.

Most of them know where to find the coffee pot and donuts and do not hesitate to serve themselves. A skillet is on the small stove in case anyone orders eggs or bacon but no one does while we are present.

We are hesitant to serve ourselves. Keith pours our coffee in a Styrofoam cup and at 40 cents it's a cheap jolt into the daylight hours.

We look around and get the idea Keith is a grandfather. Drawings in crayon by youngsters are held on the refrigerator by magnets labeled "Purdue," the university just 17 miles to the east on Ind. 26. Lest any downstate fans be unhappy at Keith's partiality, an Indiana banner is on a bulletin board, under one for Purdue, of course.

This is not your designer restaurant of a new millennium. This is the reality of a man's environment. The bulletin board holds announcement of farm auctions, deer hunting information and other items of interest to outdoorsmen. A dart board is on a wall, bags of dog food are near the door and assorted merchandise, mostly items farmers need, are for sale. The walls are paneled, the floor covered with two types of carpeting.

Early risers do not appear to be Keith's only customers. His place is open daily from 6 a.m. to 5 p.m. and again from 6 p.m. to 9 p.m. A sign notes that chili with toasted cheese will be served later, the cost $3. Milk shakes are available for $1.50, apple pie for $1.

The restroom? It's back through an aisle past the tiny kitchen and up a step.

The sun is rising. A few more men enter to join in the conversation or to read the morning *Lafayette Journal & Courier.* We leave feeling awakened by the coffee and the atmosphere. We see a hand written “Thank you” sign on the door. The visit has been our pleasure.

# OXFORD

## LOIS’ CAFE

### 109 East Smith Street

All is quiet in the town of Oxford at 7:15 a.m. on a weekday morning, but that’s because Lois’ Cafe on Smith Street in the center of town is closed temporarily.

A sign on the frame building beckons, “Good food, good friends, come on in.” We’d like to enter, but a notice in the window advises the place is closed. The cafe looks to be a typical small town cafe.

We learn later the restaurant has reopened and speak with Judy Noble, the sister of owner Lois Henry. Without hesitation, Judy describes the restaurant and its clientele of farmers, retirees and business people.

It’s a place where diners gather in the morning to share the news and dine on Lois’ specialties such as biscuits and gravy, eggs, sausage, omelets and potatoes, “the usual breakfast items,” Judy notes.

Luncheon specials are ham and beans on Mondays; country fried steak, chicken and chili on Tuesdays; an “all you can eat” salad bar on Wednesdays; meatloaf, mashed potatoes and salad on Thursdays; ocean perch on Fridays and chili and sandwiches on Saturdays. Sunday is fried chicken day.

The cafe opens at 6 a.m. daily, except Sundays when it opens at 8 a.m. It remains open until 7 p.m. daily except Tuesdays when it closes at 5 p.m. and Sundays when the doors are shut at 2 p.m.

# BOSWELL

## THE FARMER’S TABLE

### 109 South U.S. 41

Our Internet yellow pages indicate the Hometown Cafe is on West Main Street in Boswell, but, if it still is there, we do not find it.

The Farmer's Table, though, remains in town on old U. S. 41 as it has for years. The name applies to the menu and to the round table where farmers gather each morning.

It is not your usual main street diner, being in a relatively new building that stands alone back off the road surrounded by a crushed stone parking area. Only its name and the fact that most of its customers are regulars who return each morning make it different from most roadside cafes.

Not all of the customers are farmers, despite the rural reminders that hang on the walls, items like a single tree to which a horse was once hooked, horseshoes, pulleys, saws, hay cutters and horse collars.

Diners on this day include women, craftsmen, a local businessman in a suit. All seem to be regular diners, some who walk to tables at which they sit each morning day after day. Waitresses call many of them by their first names.

The breakfast menu offers the usual items. Two eggs, bacon or sausage and toast cost $2.49. Servers see that coffee cups are never empty.

The Farmer's Table is open for lunch and dinner as well as breakfast. It may not have the character and atmosphere of some Main Street diners, but the food is good on this day, as it has been each time we have stopped.

## FOWLER

### THE BENTON CAFE

**215 East 5th Street**
**(Main route through town)**

Our stop at the Benton Cafe is a bit disappointing, but that likely is not the fault of this busy restaurant.

Maybe it is because a diner at the counter ignores our greeting. Perhaps we are in a bad mood. Or it could be because the gravy on the biscuits is too spicy for our sensitive stomach.

Whatever the reason, it obviously won't stop local residents from coming here morning after morning. Or one farmer to good naturedly tell another as he leaves to "combine the hell out of them beans today." Beans and corn are big topic for conversation here for Fowler sits in the heart of some of Indiana's best farm land.

As in most small towns, everyone seems to know everyone else at the Benton Cafe and the conversations drown out the nonsense on the TV that is on. The restaurant in the core of the business district in the town of 2,300 residents is busy despite the mid-morning hour. Some customers in the 20 to 25 feet wide dining room are at the eight stools at the high counter. Others are at tables with 40 more seats.

Menus are on the tables, the breakfast items many and varied. For $3.95 diners can order "The Benton Breakfast," which includes two eggs, hash browns, toast and a choice of ham, sausage or bacon. An entry called "The Cure" includes two eggs, hash browns, two sausage patties and biscuits "all covered with sausage gravy" for $4.65."

Either item is an indication that the clientele here is mostly working people, not retirees or business folks or office workers who plan to spend the day at desks.

Fifteen different omelets are available, each with two eggs, toast and hash browns. "The Veggie," for example, includes mushrooms, onion, green peppers and black olives for $3.00. "The Benton," with ham, bacon, sausage and cheese, is $4.45.

Sandwiches, available for lunch, vary in price from $1.40 for a quarter-pound hamburger to $2.95 for a ham and cheese hoagie. Fries and slaw are an extra $1.50.

This is not a fancy restaurant. The menu and the food is more important to the people who dine here.

We may not have given the Benton Cafe a fair shake. We suggest others judge for themselves when in the Benton County seat on business or are in the area.

## MONON

### MONON FAMILY RESTAURANT

**104 East 4th Street (Just east of Ind. 43)**

It is easy to spot the Monon Family Restaurant in this northern White County town. Not many diners have a lavender and magenta front like it does.

More spacious than the average small town diner, it also is open longer hours than most. It can seat 100 or so customers and is open for all meals, starting at 5 a.m. and continuing until 9 p.m. There are no booths or stools in this roomy restaurant owned, the menu notes, by Terry and Sharon Fischer.

The dining area is being remodeled so it is difficult to get a good description of what the place may look like later.

Despite the lunches and dinners, breakfast is available at any time, the menu notes. A feature is the $3.55 "Farmer's Omelet," which includes eggs, tomatoes, bacon, cheese, mushrooms and green peppers for $3.55, almost enough food to keep a farmer on his combine until supper. All omelets are served with potatoes and toast.

For the less hungry, a breakfast of two eggs, ham, potatoes and toast is $3.45. Waffles range from $2.45 to $3.45.

The restaurant has a complete menu including a hot bar for $4.75, a salad bar for $3.95 and a senior citizen dinner for $4.55. There also is a $4.75 breakfast buffet from 7 a.m. until 10:30 a.m. on Saturdays and Sundays.

For anyone who comes to Monon to look for a place to relocate, this is a good starting point. Some of the place mats show pictures of houses for sale by Century 21.

## GOODLAND

### ROSIE'S CAFE

**U.S. 24 West**

It's not necessary to be a Purdue University sports fan to enjoy a stop at Rosie's Cafe in Goodland. It does help to be one, though.

This is a Boilermaker's paradise. The food is good and the Purdue paraphernalia obvious, even before you walk in the door.

From the outside, the little cafe doesn't look too impressive. The small frame and masonry building sits off the road, unlike older diners in old two-story buildings in the hearts of other small towns.

It's the signs in the windows that give the place a touch of flavor. A locomotive, as in Boilermaker, is painted on the window, so is another Purdue emblem. Another sign facing the parking area warns that it is "reserved for farmers, fishermen, golfers and all other liars."

An-old fashioned screen door is in place, its "Welcome" sign a greeting to visitors who enter to be faced with a "Purdue Parking Only" sign. A Purdue sweatshirt hangs on a wall, an assortment of other Boilermaker items are in place and a Purdue fly swatter is handy in case an Indiana University fan or some other pest gets out of control.

But Purdue doesn't have the only sports teams backed by the restaurant's management. It also gives support to the South Newton High School Rebel teams, which have included athletes from Goodland since consolidation three decades ago.

The dining area at the entrance is small, the ceiling so low it could be reached flat-footed by the shortest player on coach Gene Keady's Purdue basketball squad. Another eating area, off to the side, is larger, giving the cafe enough room to seat 50 diners. Tables are covered and the white paneled walls accented with pictures giving the diner a back home flavor. An air conditioner is in a window.

Goodland is small town personified. Travelers on U.S. 24 are not strangers for long, being made to feel at ease among the farmers, factory workers, retirees and businessmen and women who are regular visitors at Rosie's. The topic on this October 5 morning is an early severe frost that has just blanketed the farm country.

A man who appears to be long retired enters and is asked, "How you doin', Leroy?" Leroy's reply is brief. "Hanging in there," he says. Most of the conversation among the old-timers is about health problems. One observes what others will learn, "The golden years are not what they are talked up to be."

This is a restaurant that serves good meals without taking itself too seriously, which explains a sign that says, "Dinner will be served at the sound of the smoke alarm."

Cindy Gargano, the owner for the last 14 years, notes, "We have humorous moments every day. They (the customers) all just blend in." Diners are told, "If you're grouchy, irritable or just plain mean, there will be a $10 charge just for dealing with you."

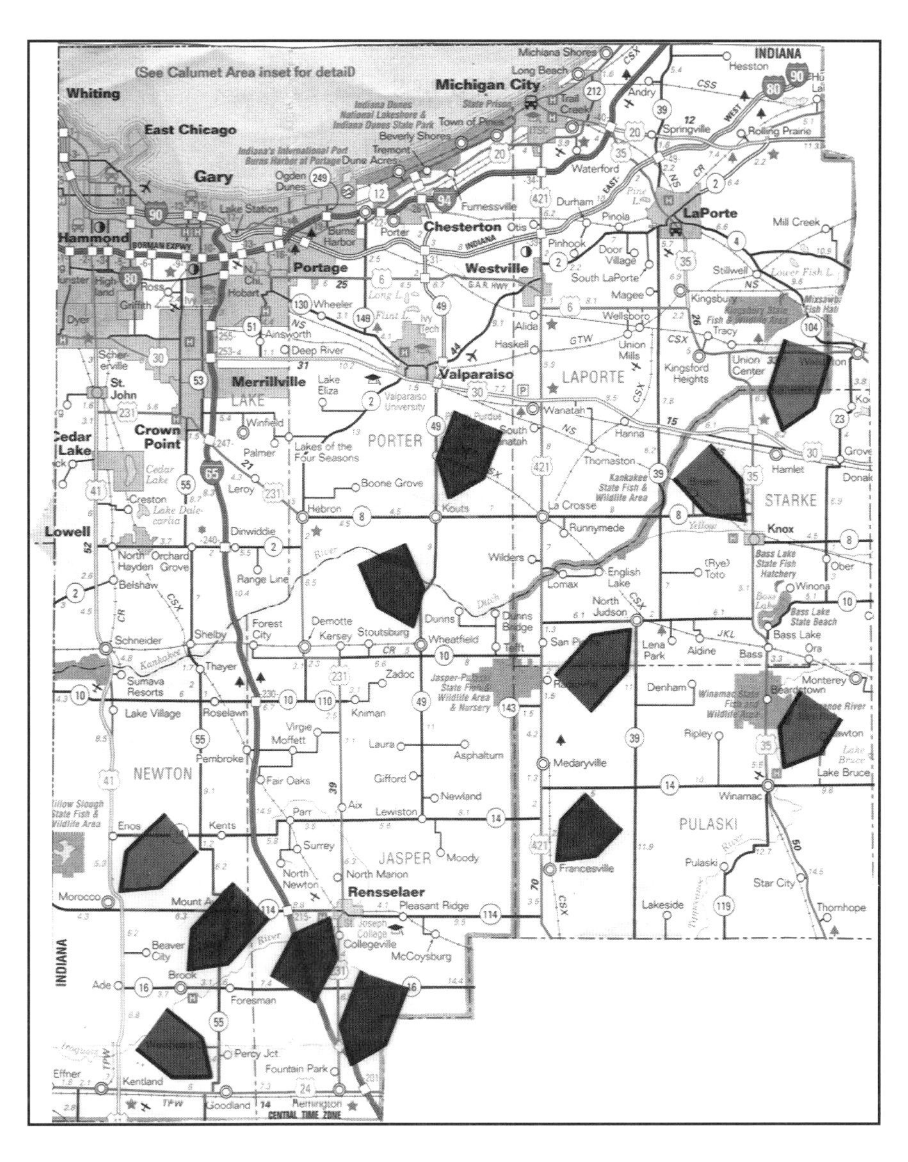


A more factual promise reads, "Great home cooking."

One pancake, we find, is almost a meal in itself. Chances are the other breakfast items are as good in taste and as big in size. Among the menu entries are two eggs, hash browns or American fries, choice of bacon, sausage or ham with toast and coffee for $3.85. Two eggs, two pancakes, choice of bacon, sausage or ham and coffee, also are $3.85.

The lunch menu includes a hamburger steak with French fries and a choice of bean salad, peaches or macaroni salad for $4.25. It can be topped off with blackberry or cherry cobblers for $1.60. "The pies, and the homemade noon specials are our specialties," Cindy Gargano notes.

"Everything we serve is homemade and we try to provide a homey place for our customers to eat," she adds.

Some places make a person feel better for having stopped. Even Bob Knight, the irascible Indiana University basketball coach, might enjoy a stop at the sunny environment Rosie's Cafe provides for rival Purdue fans.

## BROOK

### WELCOME INN RESTAURANT

**126 West Main Street**

It doesn't take long to see the Welcome Inn is owned by someone who takes pride in her business.

A visitor can tell from its appearance that this is a step above the average Main Street diner. That's obvious. The comment on the menu just makes it more so, reading:

"Betty wishes to thank all who come to the Welcome Inn. She has been in Brook for 10 years and hopes to be here many more. Her goal is to have a friendly, happy atmosphere with great food and the best service she can provide. She loves her restaurant and says thanks to all who made it possible."

Betty, we learn, is Betty Raza, the owner. Her endeavors have paid off in great food, good service and a friendly happy atmosphere.

Walk under the awning and through the door of the one-story frame building with the clapboard front and you'll be greeted as a friend by the diners as well as the waitress, who on this day is Pauline.

We have just taken a seat at one of the tables when she asks, "Coffee, dear?" Once the cup is filled she will not allow it to be empty.

The surroundings are pleasant. Venetian blinds cover the windows that look onto the street. The floor is carpeted. The walls are paneled at the bottom, plastered toward the top and accented with pictures.

Most of the men on this morning are in the front dining room, where smoking is allowed. A group of women is in the non-smoking room off to the side where the tables are covered with cloths.

They are free of the banter in which men engage . . . with each other and with Pauline. She greets a late arrival with a comment. He replies, "I don't know why I come in here. I get treated like a dog."

She retorts with the friendliness with which the comment was made, "Yeah, like a wicked stepchild, or a redhead," referring to the color of his hair.

It is another example of the friendly atmosphere as is a greeting to another arrival, "Where you been? We've been worried about you."

The breakfast menu offers a wide variety of items, all reasonably priced. Two eggs, two sausage links or patties and toast, for example, are $2.99.

A cheeseburger with fries and slaw is $4.50 at noon. Lunch plate specials are available daily. And all buns are baked fresh daily.

Betty Raza's Welcome Inn business card notes the restaurant also offers a complete catering service for banquets, reunions, picnics, weddings, graduations and parties.

Open from 6 a.m. to 2 p.m. daily, except Sundays, this is a good place to stop if you're in northwestern Indiana and would like breakfast or lunch away from fast food restaurants. It's worth a stop before a visit to the George Ade Memorial Park just east of Brook on Ind. 16.

Besides, even sophisticates like George Ade would have liked this little restaurant in his old home town. Ade (1866-1944) was the noted playwright, humorist, columnist and author who once had three hits running at the same time on Broadway.

# MOROCCO

## THE LUNCH BOX

### 215 East State Street

The Lunch Box is in a tall narrow building painted white with lace curtains on windows that face onto State Street in Morocco's business district.

It is mid-October and tables are covered with cloths featuring Halloween designs. The season also is reflected in the window decorations.

We arrive after the 2 p.m. close, but a repairman lets us glimpse inside the restaurant, which is neat and clean.

# REMINGTON

## THE REMINGTON CAFE

### 12 South Ohio Street

Forget the fast food restaurant at the intersection of U.S. 24, if you're driving on I-65 in northwestern Indiana. You can be served at your table in a comfortable restaurant in Remington a mile or so to the west.

The Remington Cafe & Bakery is not on Main Street, but it is in a one-story building, the one with the maroon awning near the railroad in the town's business district.

The cafe is neat and clean with carpeted floors, low ceilings and a farm scene border at the top of the walls. Customers may choose to sit at one of eight tables or on ten stools at the counter. Venetian blinds shut out the morning sun on the windows that face to the east.

The restaurant, established in 1972, has been owned by Carol and Harold Arbuckle since 1996. Carol's business card also notes she offers "decorated cakes for every occasion." And her sugar cookies, 50 cents each or six for $2.75, also are available.

At mid-morning we are more interested in breakfast, the menu offering a wide selection. Two eggs with hash browns and toast are $2.80, a ham and cheese omelet, $3.75. The "Farmer's Breakfast" with two eggs, two pancakes, hash browns, toast and choice of bacon, sausage or ham is $4.25. The "Country Breakfast" for $3.25 includes a half order of biscuits and gravy, one egg and hash browns.

Three pancakes, billed as "the fluffiest you'll ever eat," are $2.05. Two pancakes with two eggs are $2.20.

Today's lunch special is a cabbage roll with cheesy potatoes and green beans for $3.95. Other luncheon dinner specials include steak or shrimp with salad, choice of potato and dinner roll, each for $4.95.

For diners who don't order the specials, there is an assortment of sandwiches, such as a "Cavalier Burger" with cheddar cheese, special sauce, lettuce and tomato and chips for $3.95. We regret we are not hungry enough to try it.

A cup of soup, chicken strips and one side are $3.95, the soups this day Great Northern bean or cheesy California cream. Chili also is available. And a word about the soup. It's also available for $3 a pint or $5 a quart, which allows senior citizens to dine here at lunch and carry home their supper.

The cafe is open from 5:30 a.m. to 3 p.m. Mondays though Thursdays and from 5:30 a.m. to 8:30 p.m. Fridays and Saturdays. Lunch, Mrs. Arbuckle says, usually attracts the most customers, except on Saturdays and other occasions when they are outnumbered by those who come for breakfast.

It is, she adds, the home cooked food—"home cooked, not frozen and warmed up"—that bring farmers, retirees, construction workers and office personnel to the cafe day after day.

And the home town flavor and lack of pretense helps. There aren't many places where an elderly woman can—and once did—walk to the restroom while announcing she had wet herself.

And those customers are not forgotten, even in death. Each time a local resident dies, a jar is set out where diners may deposit money for flowers or for a charity.

We make a note to return to try the "Cavalier Burger." It'll give us a chance to dine at a home town cafe instead of ordering the Big Mac at the McDonald's out near the interstate.

# RENSSELAER

## JANET'S KITCHEN

### 112 Van Rensselaer Street

A sign on the front of Janet's Kitchen, a half block from the Jasper County Courthouse, promises this is "the place where locals like to meet."

Stop at 6 a.m. at the diner with a look similar to a Swiss chalet, and you will find it's true. An assortment of small trucks are out front, reflecting the diversity of its early diners. Most of the customers at this early hour are men, but that changes as morning dawns.

A table for six in the front dining area is reserved, a notation says, "for farmers, fishermen, golfers and all other liars." Four men qualify. They likely have been there since the restaurant opened an hour earlier and now wait for others to join them. It, incidentally, is the only table covered with a cloth.

One regular customer, however, has taken a seat at another table. A new arrival at the liar's table asks him, "What's the matter? Have you been a bad boy." The man smiles and continues to read his newspaper, which is hard to do if engaged in conversation.

Younger men, most of whom will leave in the pickups parked out front, are seated at other tables, reliving their nights and outlining their work day to come. Later in the morning, the mayor, lawyers, judges and bankers may stop by to begin their days.

A restaurant has been at the location for at least 75 years, perhaps longer. A picture of the interior of the place dates back to 1954. Janet is Janet DeLaney, the owner with Kenneth DeLaney.

Seven stools are at an L-shaped counter. About 25 seats are at tables in the front dining room. More are at tables in a room off to the side, giving the restaurant seating for 65 customers.

Janet's is a breakfast and lunch diner, the hours 5 a.m. to 2 p.m. weekdays and 5 a.m. to 11 a.m. on Saturdays. It is closed on Sundays.

Breakfast, which attracts the biggest crowd, is served until 11 a.m. It offers a variety of choice from à la carte oatmeal, $1.30, to an order of ham, two eggs, toast and hash browns for $4.40. A sausage, bacon or ham omelet with pancakes or toast is $3.90.

Three hotcakes are $2.70. The special on this day is French toast with sausage or bacon and coffee for $3.25.

For lunch the special is chicken breast, dressing and mashed potatoes for $3.95. Roast beef and shrimp are available. A grilled cheese sandwich with chili is $3.50, a beef Manhattan, $4.50. Sandwiches range from $1.90 to $3.50.

Janet DeLaney says everything is homemade, including the daily specials, the pies and the rolls. "This is a family-owned and a family-operated business with a family atmosphere," she says. "It helps us keep up with family and friends and the town happenings."

It's also a place where fun can mix with work. "A customer was teasing us one morning. When he came back for lunch, we served him a frozen scoop of mashed potatoes covered with chocolate syrup," Janet recalls. "Everyone," she adds, "got a big laugh out of that." Chances are so did the man to whom the "sundae" was served.

Give Janet's Kitchen three stars. Few, if any, customers will be disappointed with the food or the atmosphere.

## PEPPIN'S COUNTRY CORNER

### 101 East Elm Street

Peppin's is another Rensselaer restaurant that appears to be a good place to stop, although it is not in the downtown area and isn't in an old building in the business district.

It's a few blocks from downtown in its own building, one decorated for the Halloween season ahead. It, too, is open for breakfast and for lunch.

# WHEATFIELD

## SCHOOLHOUSE INN

### 139 East High Street

The address is misleading. The Schoolhouse Inn does not face East Street. It is instead on another street, just north of what looks to be a new Wheatfield Elementary School.

Once some visitors glance at the Schoolhouse Inn, they might drive off, unimpressed. If they take a closer look—especially in the morning hours—they will see the Lincoln town cars and other big sedans in front of the little white concrete block building.

Only a small sign over the door, "Schoolhouse Inn" on a red brick background, notes this is a restaurant. Lace curtains cover the small windows onto the street.

A visitor soon gets the idea there is not much formality at the Schoolhouse Inn. A small sign at the entrance notes, "Shoes and shirts are required. Bras and panties optional."

No matter! It is a place the locals congregate each morning to sip coffee, order a donut or maybe a full breakfast and exchange whatever news occurs in this northern Jasper County town.

The breakfast choices include two eggs and bacon for $3.50. Three hotcakes are $2.70. Soups and sandwiches are available for lunch.

Six men are at a table in a corner, talking about cars, crops and whatever else is mentioned. Men and women share another table, joined later by other couples who enter to jump start their days with the Schoolhouse coffee. The topic at their table is law and order. A male among the group philosophizes, asserting, "You have to fear the law to respect the law."

Two strangers are eyed, not suspiciously, but with curiosity for it is doubtful if many out-of-town diners stop here.

A single restroom has a tiny round sink, a type from an earlier time. A bar of lava soap indicates those drivers of the big cars out front worked, or still work, for a living at jobs that dirtied their hands.

If you're looking for a restaurant that is a million miles and light years away from McDonaldland, this place is worth a stop. You will find that folks in small towns don't need state-of-the-art buildings, fancy menus or elegant surroundings to enjoy each other's company over cups of coffee.

### HUDGENS HOUSE
**Ind. 10 - Wheatfield**

No more than a half-mile away from the Schoolhouse Inn, but a world apart is the Hudgens House. It is newer, much larger, likely more upscale than the Schoolhouse Inn.

It certainly isn't as hometownish. And the vehicles out front are more likely to be pickup trucks or smaller sedans.

## KOUTS

### THE KOFFEE KUP
**105 South Main**

It doesn't take long to see why the Koffee Kup is a favorite of farmers or anyone else with a rural background. Owners Tim and Donna Brown have made it a place to relive the past while talking about what has been in anticipation of what may come.

It is difficult to know where to begin to review a visit to the Koffee Kup. It could be the building. It could be the interior decorations. Or it could be the food and service.

Let's start with the building, which dates back to 1890. It was, Tim Brown says, a general store and drug store until 1954, when it became the Koffee Kup. A picture shows what it looked like back when Main Street (now Ind. 49) was unpaved and the dirt surface often turned to mud.

The building still looks much as it did then, a false front giving the appearance it has two stories instead of one. It has, however, taken on a brighter look since the Browns became owners in 1993.

"It has taken a lot of work," says Tim Brown, who has helped to give the diner a new look. The yellow brick front trimmed in blue offers a good first impression which is even more favorable once inside.

That's when you see the farm motif. A sign designates a side wall as John Deere Drive. A back wall is Allis Chalmers Drive.

The other side is International Harvester Road. Areas are designated for "Case Parking Only" or for "Allis Chalmers Parking Only." Another sign from the past reports, "McCormick Deering Farmall Sold Here."

Hundreds of model farm tractors and toy implements line shelves. Walls, in addition to the farm items, are filled with curios and knickknacks.

It is 7:55 a.m. and seven men, including one in a white shirt and tie, are at a round table, talking about farming, of course. Some have been driven in from the fields by an October thunderstorm that has brought rain that would have been of more value had it fallen before the crops matured.

One of the men mentions a comment his farmer father made a generation ago. "Yeah," he says, "I was eager to go out on Saturday night when Dad would say, 'One more row.' I think he said that every Saturday afternoon, no matter what we were doing." A visitor smiles. He recalls his dad, too, always seemed to drag out the day for "one more row."

The past, too, is reflected in the high ceiling, which is covered in old-fashioned patterned metal, the kind that was popular in the early 1900s and is now valuable as a reminder of that era. But this is about the present, not the past.

We take our gaze off the surroundings and turn to the menu which promises the Koffee Kup is "a great place to start the day." It is not an advertisement. It's a fact.

The morning special is an egg, bacon and cheese sandwich and coffee for $3.75. A very hungry farmer can order two eggs, a four-ounce rib-eye steak, potatoes, toast and coffee for $5.25. Two eggs, one pancake or potatoes, bacon or sausage, toast and coffee are $4.20.

Lunch choices include ocean perch, with potato, side dish and roll for $5.50. A three-piece chicken dinner is $4.75, the country fried steak, $4.95.

As we leave, two state officers (both females) of the Future Farmers of America enter with a sponsor, who introduces them to the men at the round table. The past has met the present, agriculture no longer the total domain of males.

The Koffee Kup seems destined to serve new generations to come. Its hours are 4:00 a.m. to 2:00 p.m. daily except Sunday.

# HAMLET

## HAMLET CAFE
**403 Railroad Street**

You won't find Shakespeare in Hamlet, but you will find the Hamlet Cafe. If you look hard enough, that is. Don't give up. You'll find the cafe, eventually. And there isn't enough traffic to make your search difficult.

Just drive north on U.S. 35 until you see the arrow to Hamlet, turn right and go to a four way stop. Turn left (north) and drive to Railroad Street. Make a left turn and go west four blocks where you will see the little diner on the right.

It is a small town cafe that isn't in the main part of town, if Hamlet has a business district. There is no sidewalk, no curb, just a parking area in front of the small one-story building. Five stools are at the small counter. Tables are set with place mats and the diner, owned by Ellen Scott, is neat and clean.

It is quiet at mid-morning, the lone waitress a college student working to become a registered nurse. A few men are at tables, rain having driven them in from their outdoor jobs.

Breakfast is served from 6 a.m. to 11 a.m. The place remains open for lunch and dinner until 8:30 p.m. weekdays, 7 a.m. to 2 p.m. on Sundays.

It is a place to order a ham and cheese omelet for $4 or try the biscuits and gravy for $1.75. The coffee is fresh, the food good.

The luncheon menu includes a hamburger steak for $4.95 or pork chops at $4.95. Desserts include carrot cake and rhubarb or peach pie.

Ash trays are on the table, but no one is smoking. There are two restrooms, both spic and span, in contrast to the unisex facilities at some other diners.

For a view of life in a small town try the Hamlet Cafe. You won't find a diner like it on fast food row in any major city.

# KNOX

## THE FAMILY CAFE

### 14 South Main Street

If you're an old sorehead when you walk into the Family Cafe in "beautiful downtown Knox," you won't be when you walk out. Rich Neuberg will see to that.

Neuberg, who owns the place with his wife, Peg, makes sure no one who enters the restaurant leaves as a stranger. He treats first-time breakfast diners as casually as he does the men and women who are there day after day. No one is immune from his comments or his banter.

"This is the place to come," he tells us. "I eat here every day myself." Head toward the restroom and he may joke, "That will cost you a quarter." It doesn't take long to get the idea that this is the ultimate in casual dining.

The cafe is in a one-story brick in Knox's old business district not far from the Starke County Courthouse. "Located two blocks west of U.S. 35 near the railroad tracks in downtown Knox," notes the menu, which promises "a dining experience," which no one will deny.

It is a downtown that has an optimistic future, Neuberg says, offsetting fears elsewhere that small town shopping districts are dead or dying. He cites the trend toward on-line Internet shopping and says shopping malls on outskirts of town could themselves be passed by in 10 years. "We'll still be here in beautiful downtown Knox which will be thriving," he promises.

Neuberg takes pride in the fact the cafe does bring people to the business district. "It's a true draw to the downtown area," he asserts.

You soon get the idea that Rich Neuberg is a walking, talking Chamber of Commerce, one who comments, not too convincingly, that he's making a "million dollars a year" at the Family Cafe. "Our families came from eastern Europe. We helped build America and make it great," he adds. It's hard to argue with a man who is proud of his heritage.

The cafe has been a fixture at the location for 40 years, owned since 1995 by the Neubergs. It's open from 5 a.m. to 3 p.m.

seven days a week, with breakfast available at anytime. “Great breakfast for the big or small appetite . . . all at great prices,” the menu reads. It is not an idle boast.

It is a wet Wednesday and most of the five stools at the counter and tables in the two dining rooms (one smoking the other non-smoking) are filled at 9:45 a.m. Rich knows most of them by their first names. If he doesn’t, he will before they leave.

Those diners can choose what is called the “Raghorn News Breakfast Special.” It is a “giant” ham steak with two eggs any style, potatoes and toast for $5.97. The “Big Band” breakfast is two pork chops, two eggs, potatoes and toast for $5.65.” Among the more routine items are a bowl of oatmeal with a toasted bagel for $2.44.

“It has been said,” the Neubergs boast, “that we have the best biscuits and gravy north of the Mason-Dixon line.”

Luncheon specials this day include liver and onions, with potatoes, one vegetable and a cup of soup for $4.00. A barbecue chicken sandwich with potato and vegetable and a cup of soup also is $4.00. Among the cafe’s specialties are ham steaks and homemade soups.

This is a small town community center, a place for locals to gather and for visitors to seek out. Diners can find seats at eight stools at the counter or at 84 seats at 44 tables in the two dining rooms. To find it, look for the Starke County Courthouse or the railroad tracks. It’s not far from either.

We leave the Knox Family Cafe feeling better. The food has been as good as promised. And we’re taking with us one of the Family Cafe caps and one of its coffee cups, compliments of the owners, as if we need a reminder of the day we visited the restaurant and talked with the Neubergs.

## NORTH JUDSON

### THE FINGERHUT CAFE

**Corner of Main and Lane**

Unlike the Fingerhut Family Bakery, which has been a Starke County tradition since 1946, the Fingerhut Cafe in back of the same two-story building, opened in early 1999.

The cafe, painted white and accented with blue awnings, is so new the place still looks neat and clean, the chairs and tables showing little wear. Halloween decorations line the walls, this being October.

This is another breakfast and lunch diner, the hours 7 a.m. to 2 p.m.

Breakfast choices include a full order of biscuits and gravy for $3.25, a half order for $2.25, a quarter order for $1.75. As expected from a bakery-related diner, the biscuits are fresh and tasty, the gravy better than at most restaurants.

Two eggs, potatoes, two slices of bacon, plus toast is $2.25. For those with larger appetites, the ham and cheese omelet (three eggs, cheese, potatoes and toast) is $4.55.

At lunch, a bowl of the soup of the day will be $2.45, a cup, $1.85. A bowl of chili is $2.95. Sandwiches include a BLT for $3.85 or a grilled chicken for $4.55.

The bakery still is too new to take on a tradition of its own. It is worth a stop, however, if you are in the North Judson area.

## WINAMAC

### MILLER'S RESTAURANT
**111 Market Street**

Were it not for the Miller's Restaurant sign out front a visitor might mistake the place for an antique shop.

In the display windows of what appears to be an old retail store are items from the past collectors would cherish. There is an old kitchen range, an ancient sewing machine and an assortment of antique furnishings.

A sign on the two-story brick building indicates it has been a fixture in Winamac since 1880. It wasn't, however, until 1998 that Liz and Jim Thompson opened the restaurant inside.

The window items are for conversation. This is a place to stop for breakfast or for lunch a half block off the Pulaski County Courthouse Square.

It is the noon hour and many of the tables in the restaurant are occupied. Diners range in age from toddlers to senior citizens, all of whom appear to be from Winamac. "Factory workers, farmers, town residents, lawyers, businessmen, we have them all," Liz Thompson says.

Miller's is more spacious than most small town diners, 30 feet wide and almost a half block deep as were most downtown stores of an earlier era. The floors are carpeted, the tables bare, the low ceiling holding fans that circulate the fresh air.

The menu is encased among three pages of advertisements for area business. A Kokomo firm, Menus Unlimited, we have learned, has printed similar menus for other small town restaurants, selling advertising to local customers. It has allowed the diners to present their items in a more attractive manner than might otherwise have been affordable.

This is a full service restaurant, with a buffet bar and daily specials that are varied enough to keep some diners returning day after day. For the less hungry, sandwiches are available.

It is where the local residents start their days with coffee at 50 cents a cup. Or with biscuits, gravy and potatoes for $4.60, a western omelet for $4.85 or a ham and cheese omelet for $4.30.

The restaurant, it appears, has in a short time become a town fixture, as much, it seems, as the 120-year-old building it occupies. Or as those antiques in the display window.

## FRANCESVILLE

### KORNER KAFE

**Montgomery Street**

We are disappointed when we find the Korner Kafe in the center of town closed. It appears to be the type restaurant every small farm town needs.

Competition, some of which no longer exists, was one reason the Korner Kafe closed. Two other restaurants, a drive-in and two pizza outlets, made survival difficult in the town of 975 residents, explained Kathy Meyer, who owned it with her husband, Robert.

Now that some of that competition is gone, the Meyers hope to find a buyer, who will reopen the cafe.

"Owning a restaurant is a tough business, but I did enjoy most of it," says Mrs. Meyer, who took over the operation in 1993.

"My greatest pleasure came," she adds, "in knowing we tried to do our best to make people happy. We catered to working people. Men with dirty boots or dirty clothes felt comfortable being here."

Now that the Korner Kafe is no longer open she can relive the moments of pleasure when it was in operation. One of those times came at Christmas one year when a local church came into the restaurant to sing carols for her mother, knowing she always dined there.

The restaurant was open from 6:30 to 2 p.m. Mondays through Fridays, 6:30 a.m. to 11 a.m. Saturdays and 7 a.m. to 2 p.m. Sundays.

Chances are the farmers, widows and business workers who stopped by each day will be delighted if the Korner Kafe reopens. This "Small Town with a Big Heart" needs a place for the locals—and for visitors—to enjoy breakfast, lunch and a Sunday buffet.

Motorists driving on Ind. 43 are advised to detour into Francesville. The Korner Kafe may have reopened when you are in the area.

* * *

A restaurant called the Elegant Farmer a half block from the Korner Kafe is open, but it appears to be more upscale than most small town diners. It does not open until 11 a.m., too late to attract men and women who want to share breakfast and friendship. It remains open until 9 p.m. daily, except on Sundays when its hours are 11 a.m. to 2 p.m.

# NORTHEAST BY NORTH

## TIPTON

### FAYE'S NORTHSIDE CAFE
**506 North Main Street**

It may take a while to find Faye's Northside Cafe, but the result is worth the search.

As the national publication *Farm and Ranch Magazine* reported when it visited the cafe, "Folks flock here for down home deliciousness and great home cooked meals."

Couples have been known to drive 35 to 40 miles, Monday through Saturday, to savor the food. And to top a meal off with one of Faye's homemade pies.

But first, some directions to the cafe, which is in an old two-story brick in a non-commercial area north of the Tipton County Courthouse. It is best to find Ind. 28, then drive north on Main Street to the red flasher light. The "Northside Cafe" sign over the sidewalk on the west side of the street will guide the way from there. You'll know you've arrived—even if it is 5 a.m.—by the cars and pickups parked nearby.

Don't be disappointed by the lack of luster on the outside. Like a good book, what's inside is more important than what's on the cover.

Inside, there are booths and tables as well as stools at a counter facing the kitchen area. An assortment of pictures, many from an earlier era, are on the paneled walls. So are what appear to be plates, antiques, perhaps, but we are not students of Chinaware. Flower baskets are in place and an old non-electric cash register is off to the side of the counter.

It is an hour before dawn and many of the booths and tables are occupied as is a stool at the counter. And more diners are en route. "The farmers will start coming in about 6 a.m.," server Theresa Louthen explains.

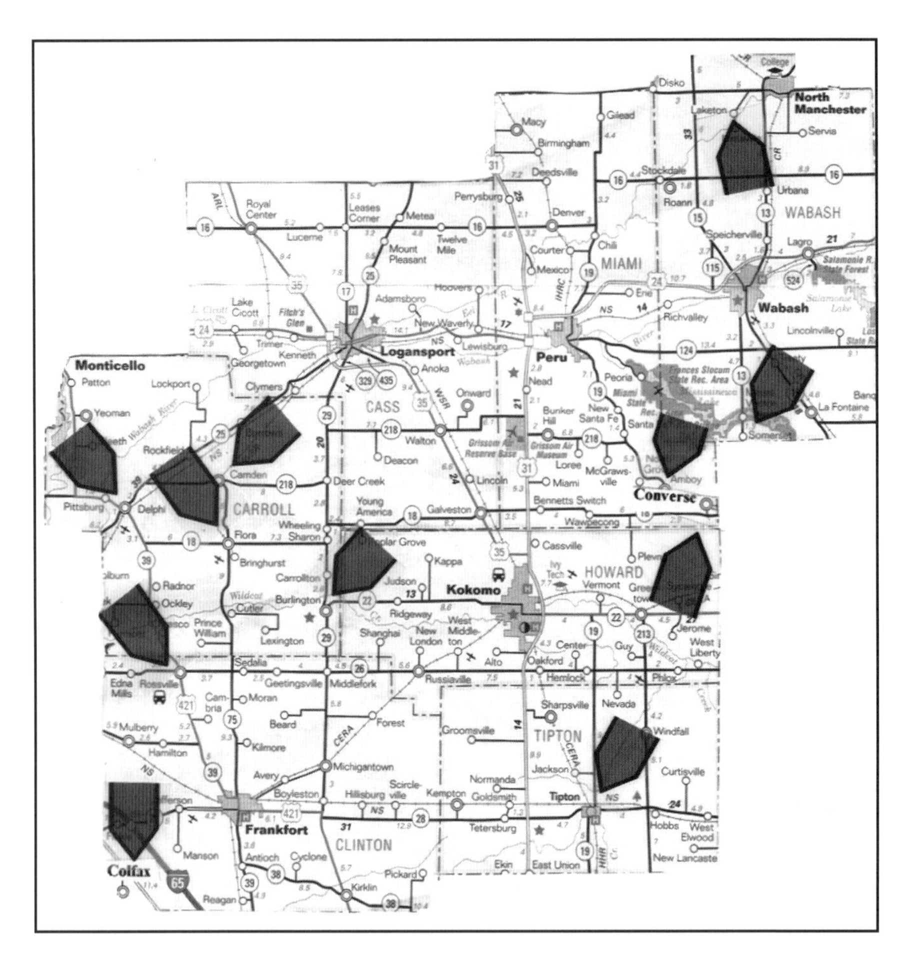


Mrs. Louthen, the mother of owner Faye Stevens, pours our coffee and adds, “Everyone here knows everyone else.” If they don’t, they likely will before they leave.

The customers call each other by nicknames such as “Granny” or “Chip” and catch up on what has happened over the last 24 hours.

One couple in the twilight of life dines alone, the man in bib overalls and a cap, the woman in a dress. They do not share in the conversation with others until they rise to leave.

A woman at another table smiles as she asks the couple, jokingly, “Are you going home to do the milking?”

The two laugh aside the question, which needs no answer. It has been years, likely, since they farmed the rich land that surrounds the town, longer still since they or other farm families kept cows for milk and chickens for eggs.

Another woman is among the men at what may be the "liar's" table. She ignores what they are saying and works the crossword puzzle in the morning paper.

The hometown atmosphere aside, it is the food that also draws customers. If a farmer doesn't plan to come in from the fields at noon, he may want to order the "Hardy Man," which is two eggs, ham, two sausages or four slices of bacon, fried potatoes, toast and coffee.

Another menu item includes three pancakes with sausage, ham or bacon with coffee and toast, $4.25. Omelets range from $3.00 to $4.50.

This day being a Monday, the noon menu includes ham and beans, corn bread and mashed potatoes for $3.95. Meatloaf with two sides is $5.80, the price of most of the complete lunches. Sandwiches, such as breaded tenderloin, also are available.

Plan to stop in the entry way as you leave. The story from *Farm and Ranch* is worth reading. And Faye's recipe for her chicken and dumplings is there for the copying.

Once you leave, you won't forget how to find your way back, even if the you needed directions the first time. This is a three-star stop you will remember.

Faye's Northside Cafe is open from 5 a.m. to 2 p.m. Mondays through Fridays and 5 a.m. to 10:30 a.m. Saturdays. It is closed Sundays. Workers who rise early to greet a 5 a.m. crowd six days a week need a day to themselves.

## COLFAX

### THE COLFAX GRILL

**201 West Main Street**

From the outside there isn't much to distinguish the Colfax Grill. It's in a two-story brick that dates back to 1913 when it was Masonic Lodge 472. If benches could talk, the 10-foot long one front could spin a million tales.

We enter the restaurant through an old screen door. Eleven tables with 50 to 60 seats are inside. There are no booths. Walls are paneled up four feet and divided from the paint above with a strip of wallpaper.

A few pictures are on the walls. Almost hidden is a photograph of a Colfax High School basketball team, known as the Hickories before the school closed and students were sent to Clinton Prairie decades ago. Newspaper clippings about area residents are on a bulletin board.

Signs note, "We accept cash," and "No shirt, no shoes and no service." An old coke machine, the kind where the bottles sat in cold water and the lids flipped off at an opener on the side, remains as a conversation piece.

Only one table, in addition to ours, is occupied, it by a man and woman having breakfast. A small television set is on near the rear of the dining area, but no one seems to be watching.

A waitress is prompt, the coffee hot, the cup refilled before it is empty. The menu includes the usual breakfast items, most of which are available any hour the restaurant is open. We do not order oatmeal, but the owners, Ward and Connie Suter, still recall humorously the morning a cook read an order as an oatmeal sandwich. "She made the prettiest oatmeal sandwich you've ever seen," they agree.

The lunch special on this day is hamburger steak, baked potato and green beans, $4.50. A rib-eye sandwich is available every day for $3.50, with a platter for $4.90. Steak night is Friday when the special is an eight-ounce rib eye steak with accompaniments for $6.50.

The Grill is open from 6 a.m. to 8 p.m. Mondays through Saturdays and 6 a.m. to noon on Sundays. The Suters say they cater to all ages, "farmers, retirees and blue collar workers," and add, "everything we cook, including the home cooked lunches, is good."

## THE CHATTER BOX
### 106 West Main

It doesn't take long to learn why the place is called "The Chatter Box." It is full of chatter on this morning, an endless banter among friends.

The restaurant is in a two-story brick with a roof that extend over the sidewalk as it does from all other businesses on this downtown block.

The front is covered with rough lumber painted a tasteful yellow.

The dining room is narrow, no more than 20 feet wide, but deep with seating for 50 diners. Stools are at the counter facing the grill.

Inside, the walls, rough lumber painted green, are lined with pictures of old farm tractors and equipment, fitting decor for this is in the heart of the northern Indiana prairie where farms are big and the land fertile.

Eight men at a round table ignore the morning news on a TV in the corner and chatter away, recalling the past when farms were smaller and Farmall H's were the choice of tractors. "They (the tractors) pulled a 7-foot disk. It took forever to cover 40 acres," recalls one of the men.

The Chatter Box is filled with customers and conversation. "Anyone need more coffee?" the friendly waitress yells, loud enough for all diners to hear even over the conversations. She finds most of the customers do want refills.

A man starts to leave. A shout of "Goodbye, Bill," echoes off the walls. "Bill" smiles at the farewell, which he likely hears each morning as he departs. There are no strangers here, which may be why it is a popular place to start the day.

A seat in The Chatter Box is a ring side to the world that is Colfax or any other small town in the Midwest. Signs out on U.S. 52 point the way to the town and the restaurant.

If you visit the Chatter Box, though, remember as the sign outside the restroom says, "Knock before entering." It's for both men and women.

# ROSSVILLE

## THE HORNET'S NEST

### 356 West Main Street

This is not your basic small town restaurant. It's at the edge of town, away from the main business district and it's in a newer free-standing building, unlike most Main Street cafes.

And it's an ice cream shop as well as a restaurant. But, like those small town diners elsewhere, it is coffee and late breakfasts that has attracted diners at mid-morning.

At 9:30 a.m. eight women are seated at one table, senior citizens enjoying each other's company. They are the counterparts to retired men who sometimes dominate the sounds of conversations at other restaurants. A few men are seated at other tables, but they aren't as talkative as the women.

The dining room is bright with a red tile floor. Walls are papered over three-feet high paneling. Three fans hang from the plastered ceiling, which has recessed lighting. The front of the ice cream serving area is lined with butterflies colored by youngsters.

It is obvious why this is "The Hornet's Nest." A hornet's nest—unoccupied, of course—hangs from the ceiling near a wall of pictures of the Hornet basketball teams that have represented Rossville High School over the years. A special notation boasts of Rossville's Sweet 16 teams that brought the town recognition back in 1969 and 1970.

Basketball is still big here in Rossville, a town that has retained its high school despite school consolidations which have stripped a sense of identity from dozens of other small communities.

Waitresses wear red T-shirts with pictures of hornets and "Hornet's Nest - Rossville, IN" lettering. Service is quick and there is no wait for a coffee cup to be refilled.

It is the usual breakfast items which bring out farmers and other early risers at 5:30 a.m. when the Hornet's Nest opens. It is, however the lunch and dinner menus that offer what owners David and Marcia Crail call their specialties. Those include breaded tenderloin, roast pork and pollock. Hand cut pork, grilled and breaded loins and pork, they note, make the restaurant different from others in the area. That, plus the ice cream shop, which is an attraction for families with children.

Dinner specials vary from chicken on Mondays, catfish on Wednesdays to perch on Fridays. T-bone steak, called the "All-American Special," is served on Thursdays.

This neat and clean restaurant is a must stop for basketball fans who want to dine, order an ice cream treat or view the pictures of Rossville High School basketball teams.

The Hornet's Nest is open from 5:30 a.m. to 9 p.m. Mondays through Saturdays and 10:30 a.m. to 9 p.m. Sundays.

## BURLINGTON

### THE DINNER BELL

**700 South Michigan**

**(Ind. 29 - Town's main street)**

If you want to meet a cross section of the folks who live in Burlington, walk into the Dinner Bell about 7:30 a.m. A lot of the residents will be there, greeting the morning and sharing their friendships.

They give meaning to the sign inside that notes, "Friends and Laughter Welcome."

The restaurant is on the west side of Ind. 29 in the small town's business district, its white building topped with a big Dinner Bell sign. A written history of the town is at the entrance. So is a notation that the restaurant has been a fixture in Burlington since 1947.

Inside, walls are paneled in maple to a height of three feet, then topped with rough lumber painted white. A border runs along the wall under the acoustical ceiling, which has rotating fans that hum in quiet harmony. The walls are decorated with crafts. Silk flowers are at each table and short lace curtains are over the tops of the Venetian blinds that dim the bright morning sun.

This is not a hole in the wall restaurant. The Dinner Bell can seat 150 diners at two dining areas in the front and in a meeting room in the rear where the Kiwanis Club and other groups meet.

Except for a man and wife, the diners on the northside are all males. Seven men at one table are talking about park improvements and other civic topics. It is a diverse group. Some of the men are wearing ties over dress shirts, some are in shorts.

A young father and his son, who appears to be about 2, take a seat nearby. They are soon joined by an older couple who dote over the toddler as grandparents normally do.

On the south side, the tables are covered with cloths. A few women are dining there, their conversation constant but subdued as is that of the men at the tables across the way.

Customers in steady streams enter the restaurant, knowing they will soon be served with food they know will be good.

Prices are reasonable for the varied breakfast items as well as other meals. All you can eat Friday night specials, for example, are $6.50. The Saturday night special, boneless catfish sandwich, is 4.45.

Owners Erin and Kelly Garrison call their ham loaf and Swiss steaks the specialties of the restaurant which attracts farmers, factory workers, retirees, professional men and women and young families.

"We try to offer home style meals with friendly country-style service," they add.

This is a restaurant for all meals, the hours 6 a.m. to 8 p.m. Monday through Saturday and 7 a.m. to 2 p.m. Sundays. It's a favorite stop for families.

Ask two parents whose daughter noted in a Sunday School class, "One of the top things I want to do the rest of the day is to dine at the Dinner Bell."

## FLORA

### THE CORNER CAFE

**1 South Center Street**

**(Corner of Main and Center)**

Walk in the entrance to the Corner Cafe and you'll see a notation: "There has always been a restaurant at this corner." Maybe not always, but at least 90 years, agree owners Steve and Linda McDaniel.

The restaurant, entered at the corner, is in the street-level floor of an old two-story brick building at the corner of Flora's business district.

Another sign reads, "When friends and family meet there is never a stranger." That's the way it is here in the Corner Cafe. A group of men are seated at a long table, glancing at the morning newspapers and commenting about the latest developments in the area.

A man and woman enter and sit down among them. The young couple at the dawn of adulthood is welcomed by men at the twilight of their lives. If there is a generation gap, it does not exist at the Corner Cafe.

A TV in the corner is on, but no one pays attention to it for this is a dull news day and the nearest weather pattern is out west and of no consequence for Flora.

Off to the side of the front dining room is a high counter that appears to once have been a bar. Its five seats are as high as bar stools.

Toys—tractors, trucks, fire trucks—line some shelves, a reminder of an earlier time where youngsters depended on something other than video games for enjoyment. A 1913 Indiana auto license tag is on display.

A menu board is surrounded by advertisements for area businesses. The menus have advertisements on the back. The coffee cups are ringed by advertisements. The servers wear Corner Cafe T-shirts, an indication that advertising is good business, be it in a small town or a large city.

We are at the Corner Cafe at a good time. Breakfast brings out the most customers. Among those here on this day are farmers, businessmen and women and retirees.

Corner Cafe breakfast specialties include whole hog sandwiches, monster omelets or an order of three eggs, bacon, potatoes, gravy and toast.

Luncheon specials also are home cooked. On the menu on this day is country fried steak, mashed potatoes and peas for $4.25. The reuben sandwich is another specialty for the noon-time diners.

The Corner Cafe is open from 5 a.m. to 3 p.m. Mondays through Fridays and from 6:30 a.m. to 12:30 p.m. Saturdays and Sundays. It is open each day of the year except on Christmas.

This is a diner that offers good food, pleasant atmosphere and a promise from the McDaniels that you will be treated as a friend, not as a stranger, when you arrive.

## CAMDEN

### GET IT AND GO RESTAURANT

**166 East Main Street**

Had it not been for the pickup trucks and the Buicks parked outside, we might have missed a good place to catch the flavor of life in Camden.

The Get It And Go is set back off the sidewalk in a small building that also houses Kimberly's Kut and Kurl Shop.

It's necessary to take a second look to see the "Get It And Go" sign. Those who overlook it miss a chance to share morning coffee with folks from around Camden. Folks like the farmer in this land of fertile fields who is depressed about low yields and low prices, the double whammy of agriculture.

Or the man who insists that if foreigners want to come to the United States and share in the wealth they ought to learn our language, not expect us to learn theirs. Or the eight women at one table who are less adamant about their beliefs and are more interested in social news than the problems of the world.

This obviously is one of the town's main gathering spots, a place to learn what is going on around the community. A sign, for examples, tells residents about a Democrat Party caucus to nominate candidates for the town council.

A soft drink vending machine is off to the side of the small dining area which is no more than 20 feet by 20 feet with seats for 25 diners. There are no stools and no counter.

Despite the lack of space, there is enough room for customers to dine at breakfast or return at lunch for the fried chicken.

Rather than "Get It And Go," we recommend visitors get "it," sit down, stay awhile and catch up on what's happening around this Carroll County town of 600 residents.

And don't mind the sign near the cash register that reads: "This is not Burger King. You don't get it your way. You take it my way or you don't get the damned thing." Chances are you will get your order the way you want it.

# DELPHI

## THE SANDWICH SHOP

### 112 East Main Street

This is another restaurant that can easily be overlooked. It's on the street level of a stucco-covered two-story building that borders an alley.

The wood front is painted blue. A sign, "The Sandwich Shop" hangs over the sidewalk. The dining room is small with just one table and ten to twelve stools around a horseshoe-shaped counter, all of which are filled at 9 a.m.

The grill is in view, allowing diners to watch their orders—or at least part of them—being prepared.

Two women diners, when not scratching their instant non-winning lottery tickets, are giving the waitress advice on what paint to use on the walls of her rooms at home.

A sign alerts customers, "The short order cook also is short tempered." She isn't in bad humor today. A customer leaves, telling everyone in the small diner, "You folks have a good day." She responds for all of them. "You, too, Rex."

Another customer enters and she asks, "Your usual?" The customer responds, "Yep! One pancake."

The menus are as big as the diner. Assorted sandwiches and dinners are on the menu.

One wall is a bulletin board of sorts with notice of upcoming events attached. A Delphi Lions Club broom, for sale for $8, is on display on a wall.

There is nothing elaborate about the Sandwich Shop, but it seems to please its clientele.

# CONVERSE

## HERSCHBERGER ESSEN HAUS

### 223 North Jefferson Street

Pick up the book matches with the Essen Haus name on the cover and you'll see a promise of "home cooking that can't be matched" and a promotion for "batter fried fish on Friday."

The Herschbergers' business cards note the restaurant is "where you can always find the best home cooked meals and baked goods."

There must be truth in advertising. Unlike many other small town restaurants, the Essen Haus, owned by Freeman and Ruth Herschberger, is open for three meals a day, except for Sundays. The seating is extensive, both in the front dining area as well as a room to the rear.

Like other diners, though, it too is in an old two-story brick, with a wood front painted red with white trim. Inside, fans are on the high ceiling which is supported by exposed wooden cross beams. The floor is carpeted and the tables and chairs are made from quality wood. The place is clean and neat.

It is 7:30 a.m. and five men and one woman are at the round table, where locals gather each morning. A few other tables are occupied, the occupants enjoying the Essen Haus breakfasts which are served until 11 a.m.

And what breakfasts they are. Order the "Sampler Platter" and for $6.95 you'll get two eggs, one hotcake, hash browns, a half order of biscuits and gravy, two pieces of bacon, a sausage patty and coffee. The "Farmer's Breakfast" includes two eggs, hash browns, a half order of biscuits and gravy, grilled tenderloin and coffee.

If anyone is hungry after meals like that he or she can return for lunch when specials like meatloaf, potatoes and two sides are served for $4.95, the same price as barbecued ribs, potatoes and two sides. A breaded tenderloin sandwich is $3.50.

Nightly dinner specials include "all you can eat" chicken with two sides and homemade bread ($6.95) or "all you can eat" fish with the two sides and homemade bread ($6.50). The Saturday night special is prime rib, the cost $8.95 to $12.95, depending on the size.

Diners can top off the meal with Ruth's "famous homemade pies," the flavors peanut butter, chocolate, coconut, banana or butterscotch, $1.75 per slice, $2.25 á la mode. The apple dumplings are $1.95.

No matter the time of day—from 6 a.m. to 8 p.m.—the Essen Haus has a meal that should please your taste. It's three blocks north of the four-way stop on Ind. 18.

# AMBOY

## STEPLER'S FAMILY RESTAURANT
### 116 South Main Street

The building has changed, but the food and service at Stepler's Family Restaurant in this Miami County town hasn't.

The owners and the customers have seen to that. When fire destroyed the old two-story brick that was one of Amboy's oldest buildings, a new one was built through a community-wide effort.

Owner Gary Stepler explains, "It (the restaurant) was rebuilt after a recent fire through donations of love, money, prayers and physical labor by the ones I now serve. The 'family' in Stepler's Family Restaurant includes them all."

Gary and Phyllis Stepler estimate that a restaurant has been on the site for 130 years, most of that time in the old two-story brick landmark that was a place for railroad workers to shower, dine and sleep when they stopped over in Amboy.

A picture of that building is among the old photographs on display on the gray walls in the new frame one-story building with a roof over a narrow porch on the front.

More than 60 customers can be seated, along with four toddlers, who can dine at a tiny table if they choose. That table is near a bookcase that contains stories of interest to toddlers. Volumes for older readers are in bookcases elsewhere.

Stepler's is a popular stop for farmers, businessmen and women, retirees and senior citizens. For older diners, the Steplers serve half orders and half portions. "It's something most restaurants do not do and it is, " Gary Stepler says, "appreciated by our seniors who just can no longer eat full meals. It allows them to dine at reasonable prices."

Fifteen "members" of "the family" already are in Stepler's Family Restaurant at 7 a.m. on this October Monday. Four more men are at another table, a woman and two youngster who are dining before school are at a third. Four men are at the round table, where one of them directs the conversation about the Amboy of an earlier time. Chances are on another day someone's mind will rewind to 1940 when coach Albert Conner's Amboy High School Pirates won the school's only basketball sectional title. Small town success stories never die.

Among the breakfast items are a ham, sausage or bacon and cheese omelet with toast, $2.75. Two pancakes and sausage, bacon or ham is $2.95, the same price as two waffles and sausage, bacon or ham.

Daily lunch platters, served with potato, salad and rolls, are $4.50. The unlimited salad bar, which includes two sides, is $3.25.

But back to breakfast. Biscuits and gravy also are available and have been known to be made to order. Gary Stepler recalls this incident: "A fussy man years ago said he loved the sausage gravy, but complained about the big chunks of meat. One day, being the smart-aleck I am, I removed all the sausage and served him plain white gravy. Boy did that backfire. He loved it so much he requested it that way every day."

You can't get that kind of service at many other "family" restaurants.

## SOMERSET

### DEBI'S CAFE

**5 Shopping Center**

Debi's Cafe is not in an ancient building in an old town. There are no century-old structures in Somerset, a community which was relocated in the mid-1900s to make room for Mississinewa Lake.

Debi's is, instead, in what looks like a strip mall in the rebuilt town on the west side of Ind. 13 at the southern tip of Wabash County.

Debi Chittick opened the restaurant in 1995 and has seen it grow from one dining room to two, mainly because of the big crowds the cafe attracts on Fridays and Saturdays. Each room has twelve tables with a total of 110 seats.

Debi's is open from 7 a.m. to 8 p.m. Tuesdays through Saturdays and 8 a.m. to 2 p.m. Sundays. It is closed on Mondays.

Farmers, construction workers and teachers are among the breakfast diners. Later in the day, the diners may include, Ms. Chittick notes, housewives, business people, politicians, policemen and firemen. At least one Indiana governor has been spotted among the visitors.

The breakfast menu includes three types of omelets—cheese, ham and western—the prices from $3.50 to $4.50. All are made with three fresh farm eggs and come with toast or biscuit. Other combinations with eggs are available as are pancakes, French toast, oatmeal, biscuits and gravy or hash browns or American fries with gravy.

Visitors can make their own selections at a breakfast bar from 7 a.m. to 11 a.m. on Saturdays and Sundays.

Debi Chittick lists hand-breaded tenderloins and home cooked daily specials as the cafe's specials. Dinners include chicken livers and onions, pork chops, chicken strips, rib-eye steak ($9.95) and ham steak, which include tossed salad, potato and bread.

"Our home cooked meals, friendly service at a fair price and the customer friendly atmosphere make the place different from other restaurants in the area. Everyone here works hard to provide quality food and friendly service in a clean atmosphere."

She is a cafe owner who appears to enjoy the work. "I like meeting the people, working with my employees and trying new recipes. I'm probably one of the few people who goes on vacation and gets homesick for my employees and my customers."

# LAKETON

## MARTY'S BLUEBIRD CAFE

### 15 Main Street

A sign out front still notes this is Earl's Place, but after one step inside you know the restaurant doesn't belong to a man. A woman's touch is apparent.

My traveling companion notes the "cute little" curtains on the old windows and the bluebird motif which seems to dominate the redecoration that has taken place.

It is obvious why the new owner renamed this Marty's Bluebird Cafe after she took over the business in September, 1999. Blue birds dominate a border on the wall. Crafts such as imitation bird nests and feeders are on display.

Excuse the pun, but it could be said that cafe has become Martha Huffman's Bluebird of happiness. She and Bart Huffman bought the cafe in this northwestern Wabash County town in mid-1999 and gave it a new look.

A pie pan collection is on display atop the shelves on each side amid the reminders that this is the fall season and Halloween is just two weeks away.

My companion could spend the day just admiring the motif. I'm more interested in the menu, which notes the Bluebird is open six days a week from 6 a.m. to 3 p.m. but "never on Sunday."

Had we arrived for breakfast we could have ordered two eggs with bacon or sausage and toast for $2.85. Three pancakes are $3.00; biscuits and gravy $2.50.

Available for lunch on this day are ham steak, scalloped potatoes and cole slaw for $4.50. A shrimp basket with cole slaw and French fries is $6.00. The cheeseburger deluxe is $2.95.

We order the broccoli soup. It is far above average. On other days we could have tried the cafe's specialties which are meatloaf and beef and noodles.

The decor is not the only thing of which "Marty" Huffman boasts. "Not many places offer good home cooked meals. There is no fast food here," she asserts.

She appears to have adjusted quickly to life as a restaurant owner. "The people in the community have really welcomed us with open arms. It is nice to hear their comments about the food and the atmosphere. We've made this a homey place, one where people gather. You see them in the morning and then again later in the day. I enjoy all the stories that are told, all the joking and the good time we all have.

"A lot of people come in as strangers, but you know them as friends when they leave," she adds.

To find the Bluebird Cafe it is necessary to find North Manchester. To reach Laketon, go west on Ind. 114 from the Ind. 13 intersection for about a mile, turn south (left) at the Laketon sign and drive another mile or so into the small town. The Bluebird Cafe is on the northeast corner where Main intersects with Lake Street.

It's in the building with a porch and a wooden wheelchair ramp. And a trim of blue, as in blue bird.

## ROANN

### BRIDGEVIEW INN

**Chippewa Road**

Another big restaurant in a small town is the Bridgeview Inn on Chippewa Road in downtown Roann.

Its advertisements boasts it has been "a family affair since 1982" and calls attention to its "home cooking."

Daily specials are available in the restaurant which is open from 5:45 a.m. to 9 p.m. Fridays and Saturdays and 5:45 a.m. to 8 p.m. Sundays through Thursdays.

Don't worry about visiting Roann on a day the Bridgeview Inn is closed. It's open "every day of the year," the ads point out.

## AKRON

### THE FARMER'S DAUGHTER

**105 East Rochester**

**(Ind. 14 - Akron's main street)**

Okay, so the name outside on the outdated root beer sign says this is the Akron Cafe. Believe, instead, another notation that calls it the Farmer's Daughter Cafe. Has been since 1980, "twenty years come July, 2000," says owner Patty Schultz.

Mrs. Schultz identifies herself as "Grumpy Granny" and says her daughter, Charlotte Hammond, has worked at the corner cafe for 25 years, "ever since she was 15 years old." It doesn't take long to know that the label "Grumpy Granny" is not a reflection of the real Patty Schultz.

She is far from grumpy on this day as she greets customers, serves breakfasts, and tell us about herself and her business.

The restaurant, she admits, "is a front." That confession doesn't detract from the fact that this is where folks in Akron who want to eat out come for coffee and breakfast, the "home cooked" kind, the menu notes.

At 7 a.m. on this day, some of those folks are at the "neighborhood" table toward the back talking about Y2K problems that could arise on January 1, 2000. They conclude it is a topic for conversation, not fear.

These are people who have known each other for years. A late arrival is greeted with, "Here comes the mayor." He is no mayor. He is just being razzed about his picture which has appeared in a newspaper.

It is Mrs. Schultz's customers that make the long hours—from 5 a.m. to 2 p.m.—worthwhile. "I do love the people who come here," she says convincingly.

She has been at work since 4:30 a.m. "The customers," she explains, "get upset if I don't have the doors open by 5 a.m." She is wearing a cap with chicken feathers plus a feather from a crow, she found on her farm. Anyone who looks for pomp and formality has come to the wrong diner.

The breakfast menu includes two eggs, bacon, potatoes, toast and coffee, $3.52. Omelets range from $1.25 to $3.95. One pancake is 50 cents, with coffee, $1.00. A fast food restaurant might have trouble competing in price or in service with the Farmer's Daughter.

Lunches at $4.50 include country fried steak, ham, chicken strips, shrimp or perch. Each entree comes with bread, potato, vegetable and one side dish. The special on this Monday is meatloaf.

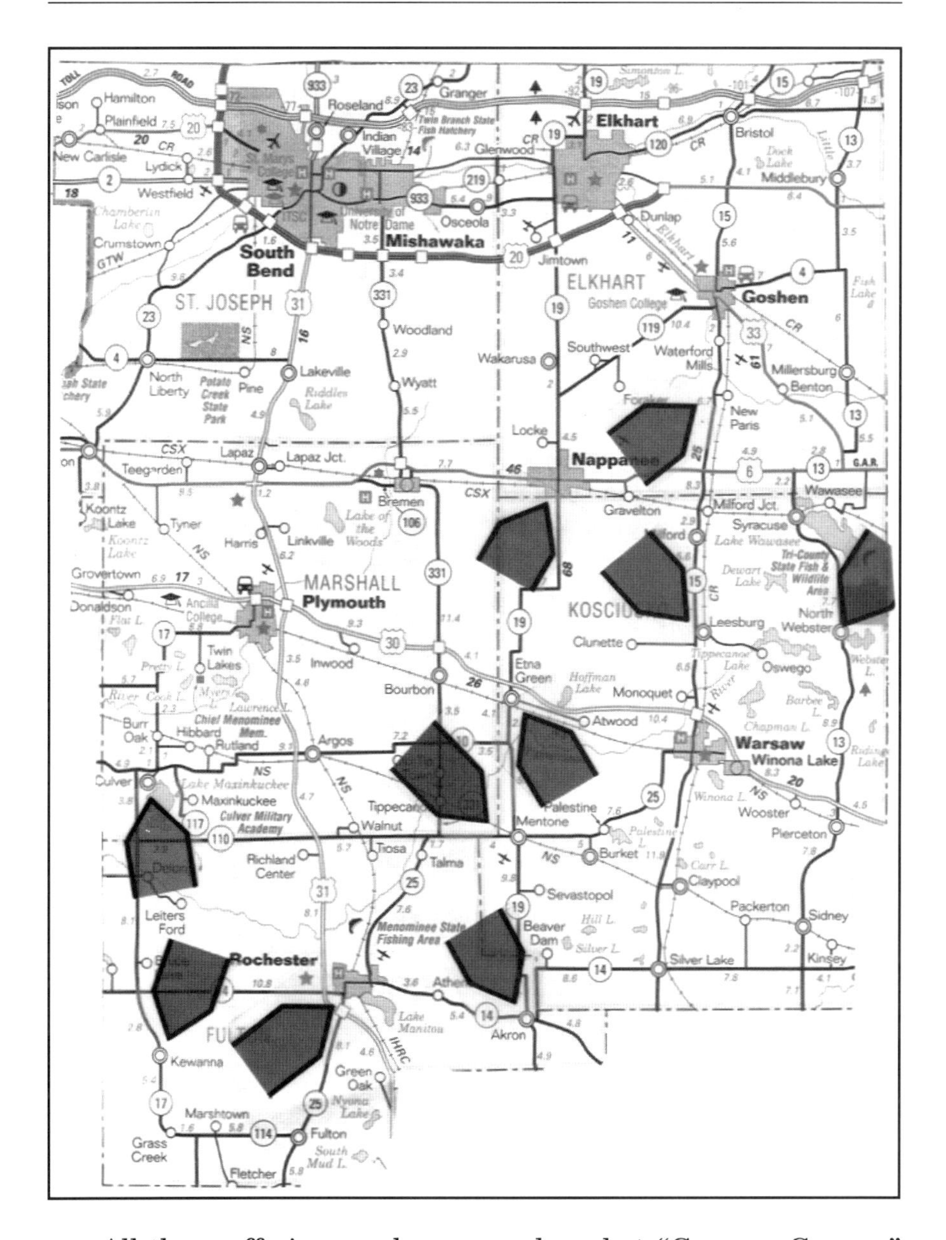


All those offerings make us wonder what "Grumpy Granny" meant by this restaurant being "a front." We get a hint, though, by looking around the cafe which has five stools at a small counter and enough booths and tables to seat 30 more diners.

Drawings by students at the local elementary students cover one wall. One of them is a picture of the inside of the restaurant, which obviously pleases Mrs. Schultz.

Debbie and Becky Clark's Heart to Heart Blossom Shoppe shares part of the dining room. Crafts and shirts are for sale as are books, which are stacked on one table that could otherwise be used by diners. Debbie and Becky are friends of Mrs. Schultz.

A small hand-written note among the items on a wall reads, "Good morning. This is God. I will be handling all your problems today. I will not need your help. Have a good day."

This is, we realize, what Mrs. Schultz means when she says the restaurant is a front. It is a place for her to share her artistic ability, her creative efforts and her views of life.

And add publishing to her talents, which also include cook, waitress and dispenser of good will. On sale at the Farmer's Daughter are a series on "Christianity in A Nutshell" and other Christian booklets hand written and designed by Mrs. Schultz. Books also are for sale.

Try finding all these things at a McDonald's or Burger King. You won't find any teen-age employees at those places with as much zest for life as Patty Schultz, the self-proclaimed "Grumpy Granny."

## ROCHESTER

### EVERGREEN CAFE

**530 Main Street**

Most of the parking places near the Evergreen Cafe are filled with pickups and sedans at 6 a.m. on a Monday morning.

It is a true indication it is a diner that remains popular after 60 years in the same corner location, the last 27 years under Jim Tyler's direction.

Tyler, only the second owner, seems to be as much a part of Rochester as the Fulton County Courthouse down the street. He's a community booster whose volunteer efforts have been recognized by the town and the Eagles Lodge. Plaques noting those awards are on display inside.

The cafe is in an old two-story building, with brown paint on the wood and bricks at the street level. Louvered vertical slats keep out the morning sun at the east windows.

It's not the appearance or the decor that draws diners day after day. It is the small town atmosphere, one where laborers and professional folks can feel comfortable in the relaxed surroundings.

As at most small town diners, this one, too, is narrow and long, a half-block deep it appears. A rubberized mat runs down the center between tables, covering part of the well-worn tile. Old fluorescent lights are on the ceiling. The yellow walls are lined with pictures that look to our non-artistic eyes to have been salvaged from yard sales. Art being art, however, the pictures may be priceless.

One picture, though, shows a horse and wagon with a "will deliver" sign. It is a reflection of the cafe's long history that began when T. A. Murphy was the driver and the business phone number was 183.

The kitchen is off to one side in a rounded area away from the front section. At this early hour most of the 20 stools that face toward the kitchen are filled with diners. Many of the eleven tables are occupied, mostly with men—farmers, factory works and businessmen—although a few women are among the diners.

Among the breakfast items are a bacon, sausage or ham omelet for $3.75, oatmeal, $1.85, or two pancakes, $1.65. Coffee is 75 cents a cup.

The luncheon special is roast pork and dressing, mashed potatoes and gravy, corn, fruit and bread for $4.75. Chili is $1.95. Among Tyler's specialties are those homemade daily specials, the pies and tenderloins.

The restaurant is open from 5:30 a.m. to 2 p.m. It is the early opening, and the old-fashioned atmosphere, that makes the Evergreen Cafe different from other Rochester restaurants.

If you're into pencils you may want to ask Jim Tyler about his collection. As a member of the American Pencil Collectors' Society, Tyler has about 12,000 ink pens, according to a newspaper feature.

## ALEJANDRA'S FAMILY RESTAURANT
### 719 Main Street

It really isn't fair to compare Alejandra's with the Evergreen Cafe up the street as far as the breakfast crowd is concerned. It is a different type restaurant, although it too is open for breakfast at an early hour.

While the Evergreen is busy, Alejandra has only a few customers. Being a three-meal a day restaurant, its main business comes later in the day.

Alejandra's is a neat place, one whose spaciousness is betrayed by the small, unpretentious, entrance off Main Street. The inside is much more attractive than it might appear from outside. The floor is carpeted, the ceiling is vaulted, the booths large, the aisles wide and uncluttered. Another dining area is off to the side of the kitchen area.

Those who opt to have breakfast here can select what the menu calls the "Country Breakfast." It includes two eggs, bacon, ham or sausage, hash browns, two hot cakes and coffee for $5.95.

The restaurant offers full lunch and dinner selections with steaks and fish, the seafood "direct from the ocean," the menu promises.

Diners also may want to try the "Alex" hamburger, "served open-faced with lettuce, mayo, French fries and cole slaw or salad." And for dessert, the hand-dipped milkshakes are a rarity in these days of fast food restaurants.

When in Rochester, you may want to have breakfast at the Evergreen, then stop at Alejandra's later.

# KEWANNA

## LYNN'S COFFEE SHOP
### 118 Main Street

It is noon on a Wednesday and many of the tables are occupied with farmers, retirees and men and women who work in town.

We are too late for the morning clientele, which starts its day with coffee and breakfast—and good humor—at Lynn's.

This is a typical small town diner in a one-story building with a green paneled front. A hardware store is on one side, *The Observer* newspaper office on the other.

Inside, the lights are recessed in a low ceiling. Tile covers the floor and the walls are paneled to a four-foot height, then painted. It appears to be a place customers are more interested in food than in appearance.

The lunch menu offers a variety of options. Pot roast is $4.00. A two-piece chicken dinner is $3.95, the barbecue sandwich platter, $3.95, and the grilled tenderloin platter, $4.50.

As at most small town cafes, there is humor at Lynn's. A sign near the cash register warns, "I can only please one person a day. Today is not your day. Tomorrow doesn't look too good, either."

Lynn's is open from 6 a.m. to 2 p.m. except Monday when it is closed.

# CULVER

## CAFE MAX

### 113 South Main Street

Step into the Cafe Max and you get a glimpse of Culver's past as well as its present. It, we soon find, is one of Main Street Indiana's best diners, certainly one of the top five we will visit.

Susan Mahler, as owner for the last fifteen years, has made the cafe an attraction for both visitors and local residents.

Visitors are drawn to Culver by Lake Maxinkuckee and the storied Culver Military Academy, which attracts students from throughout the country. And like it does the locals, the "Max" lures the out-of-towners with good food, a pleasant atmosphere and a collection of memorabilia that adds to its ambiance.

On this late autumn day the clientele is diverse. There are retirees, young mothers with small children, businesswomen, businessmen and men who work with their hands. All blend into the serene setting that is quieter than at most small town cafes.

Cafe Max is in an old two-story building that looks as if it could have once been a retail store. A green awning accents the front and covers part of the sidewalk. Mums are in bloom near two benches and umbrellas cover tables for outdoor dining on warmer days.

But it is the inside that makes for conversations and observations. The ceiling is at least 20 feet high and covered with the old-fashioned patterned metal, the type once common in general stores and other buildings in the early 1900s.

Walls are lined with pictures of graduating classes from Culver High School as well as some of its basketball teams. Memorabilia from the Culver Military Academy includes a reminder of its famed Black Horse Troop's appearance at the 1977 presidential inauguration in Washington. Various military uniforms are on display.

Small towns sometimes make visitors seem like outsiders. Says Susan Mahler, "We want them to feel comfortable and our memorabilia helps to spark conversation among our customers and our staff."

A ledge about 12 feet up the walls is lined with trophies and flower pots. A heating duct runs down the center of the restaurant, but it seems to add, not detract, from the atmosphere.

Smoking and non-smoking sections are in the long, narrow restaurant, which has tables, booths and eight stools at a counter near the back. The tables are covered and the floor is carpeted.

An upstairs dining room, which can seat another 48 diners, is used in summers when more people are in the lakeside town.

Specialties are home-baked raisin and wheat breads and cinnamon rolls for breakfast, which draw the most customers in summer months. In the winter, the lunch crowd is larger, drawn to Cafe Max by homemade soups and the friendly staff. The daily number of customers ranges from a winter low of 50 to a high of 400 in the summer.

The luncheon special on this day is augraten potatoes, ham, green beans and bread for $3.95. The soups are cream of chicken and beef cabbage.

Hours are from 6 a.m. to 2 p.m. seven days a week, with lunch starting at 11 a.m.

The menu notes: "Since 1985, our goal has been to provide the best food and service in small town atmosphere. We are always trying to improve and welcome your suggestions."

A Culver native, Ms. Mahler bought the cafe at age 22. She credits a customer for the suggestion that memorabilia be used to redecorate the place and adds, "It is a work in progress still. And it probably won't end till the day I sell or die!

"As for the community there are three facets: The town, the lake and the academy. I include all in the decorating.

"It really depends on what time of the year you are here as to the impression you will get from your visit. The winter is a sleepy time. Without industry the only people you'll see at the cafe are the local business owners and a few construction workers."

She calls the military academy (a private boarding school for girls and a military academy for boys, grades 8-12, with an enrollment of 750 in winter and 2,000 in the summer) "a great school, which we are very fortunate to have it in town. The visiting families of the students give a huge boost to the local economy."

Anyone in town on summer weekends may spot a few celebrities who are in town because of the academy. But the staff at Cafe Max, and most of the locals, let them enjoy their desire for privacy.

Out front the restaurant on any summer weekend a 1978 Pinto may be parked in front of a 1999 Jaguar. If you look in the cafe, you may have a hard time telling which man is driving which car. "The only thing that might give it away," Susan Mahler explains, "is the six-carat diamond on the wife's or girl friend's hand."

No matter whether you drive a Jaguar or a Pinto or accompany a mate with a big diamond you'll be treated royally at Cafe Max.

## MENTONE

### TEEL'S FAMILY RESTAURANT

**108 West Main Street**

Teel's is not a typical small town diner. It is instead, in size and in menu, a big family restaurant in a free-standing masonry building that extends for a fourth-block on Main Street.

For a town of 900 to 950 residents it is large and obviously an attraction for diners throughout the area.

Its advertisements, which note that Jim Apostolis is the owner, give some indication that Teel's is more than a Main Street diner. Those ads note that reservations are accepted and that a banquet room is available.

It was our misfortune to find it closed, as it is always on Mondays. Had we been in town on any other day, chances are we would have seen the locals gathered for breakfast which is served from 6 a.m. to 11 a.m.

A luncheon buffet with salad bar is available from 11 a.m. to 3 p.m. from Tuesdays through Sundays. The restaurant is open on Fridays and Saturdays when dinner buffets, as well as the regular menu, are available until 9 p.m.

## ETNA GREEN

### ETNA GREEN CAFE
**112 West State Street**
**(Old U.S. 30)**

An indication of the popularity of a small town diner is the number of vehicles outside. It is 8:30 a.m. and six pickup trucks, four vans and five cars are parked at the Etna Green Cafe.

The food obviously is the reason. There is nothing unusual or especially attractive about the brick building with a crushed stone off-road parking lot. A windbreak entrance provides space for a community billboard.

Two dining rooms are inside, the floor of the front covered in tile, the walls painted. It appears to be a smoking area. The other room, apparently for nonsmokers, has a carpeted floor, paneled walls and ceiling fans. Men occupy the front room, women and a few men the other.

It is a diverse group, farmers, retirees, men who work at various occupations. Some of the men at the counter are talking about the restoration of old tractors. Two others are wondering if the state police helicopter seen in the area was trying to spot illegal bird hunters or was in search of marijuana plants.

This is not a place that takes itself too seriously. A sign notes, "If you don't like my cooking, lower your standards." Another warns, "Contrary to popular opinion, God's name is not damn."

So much for all that. This is a restaurant and restaurants are about food. Owner Vance Stills' menu promises "good home cooking" and offers numerous selections to back up the comment. Among the varied breakfast choices are a ham and cheese omelet for $3.65, or a western omelet for $4.50. Coffee is 57 cents (60 cents with tax) and there seems to be no limit on refills.

The lunch specials on this day are broasted chicken, broasted chops, barbecued ribs or Swiss steak, each with potato, salad and roll for $5.75. Other homemade specials with the same additions are in the $4.75 range.

Despite the sign, you won't have to lower your standards to like the cooking. To find out for yourself stop at the cafe the next time you are in Etna Green. It will be the restaurant near all the pickup trucks, vans and cars.

The Etna Green Cafe is open from 5 a.m. to 8 p.m. Mondays through Saturdays and 5 a.m. to 2 p.m. on Sundays.

### MOM'S CAFE
**111 Walnut Street**

A few blocks from the Etna Green Cafe and nearer the Etna Green business area is Mom's Cafe.

Mom's is open from 6 a.m. to 3 p.m. Sundays through Wednesday and from 6 a.m. to 8 p.m. Thursdays through Saturdays.

## NAPPANEE

### CORNER CAFE
**161 South Main**
**(Corncr of Main and Lincoln)**

The Corner Cafe in this Elkhart County town offers food for thought as well as for nourishment. The first thing diners see when they sit down at tables are place mats with 25 "Thoughts for Today." Among them are:

*"Thoughtfulness is to a friendship as sunshine is to a garden."*
*"Pray for a good harvest, but continue to hoe."*
*"We cannot direct the wind, but we can adjust our sails."*

*"It takes both rain and sunshine to make a rainbow."*
*"You are what you have learned from the past, what you experience today and what you dream for tomorrow."*

You get the idea. The thoughts are something to consider while sipping a 57-cent cup of morning coffee and checking the menu in the small diner. As the name reflects, it's on the corner of Main (Ind. 19) and Lincoln, just a block south of U.S. 6, the main traffic artery through town.

The restaurant, part of a two-story brick building, has eight chairs at a counter and enough table room for 50 or so customers. The blue walls are decorated with flowers. Jars and glassware sit on shelves near the ceiling from where fans gently circulate the air.

At mid-morning, five men are at a table toward the rear, swapping stories and checking on each other's well being. What appear to be five career women are at another large table near the front. They are previewing the day ahead.

This is a home town restaurant with homemade goodness, such as homemade bread and homemade ice cream as well as a homemade menu entry called "the haystack." A "haystack," a pleasant waitress tells us, "is hash browns topped, in order, with grilled onions, two scrambled eggs, a slice of cheese, sausage gravy and cheddar."

But that is far from the only breakfast item offered by the cafe owned by Robert and Marsha Thomas. Diners may also choose between baked or regular oatmeal, sausage gravy over hash browns or the day's breakfast special, which is two scrambled eggs, two sausage links, potatoes and toast for $3.55. A ham and cheese on a bagel is $2.35.

Breakfast is served from 6 a.m. until 10:45 a.m. If you are in town for the day, it might be well to return for lunch which is available until the 2 p.m. close. Lunch includes an assortment of sandwiches and entrees. The homemade ice cream in flavors like black cherry, chocolate mousse, peppermint and butter pecan is 75 cents a dip.

A sample of one or more flavors will give you time to memorize some more of those "Thoughts For The Day," unless you can obtain a copy to take with you.

# NEW PARIS

## FRIENDS CAFE
### 68457 Main Street

New Paris, population 1,000, isn't a big town but you have to look closely to find its one diner. Only a small "Friends Cafe" sign indicates the small building back from the sidewalk is a restaurant.

Vines cover the posts that support the roof over the porch of the building that is connected to a two-story brick building that houses the Pro Hardware Store.

Inside, the restaurant's walls are paneled to a height of four feet, then painted to the acoustical tile ceiling. Pictures are on the walls. A sports calendar for Fairfield High School teams is on display, New Paris being a part of that consolidation with Millersburg. There are seats for 44 customers.

We, unfortunately, arrive at a quiet time, having missed the banter of coffee drinkers who likely were there earlier. Only two other customers are present at 10 a.m. when breakfast is still being served.

Had we been at Friends earlier we might have seen owner Jayne Tyler step outside to serve George and Roy, two of her favorite customers. They are dogs, pets which accompany two customers to the restaurant each morning.

"I make each dog an egg on toast sandwich," explains the owner. Try getting that kind of service at a fast food outlet.

The special on this morning is an egg, meat and cheese muffin for $2.25. Two eggs, sausage and toast is $2.50. A ham and cheese omelet is $3.95, a western omelet $4.25.

At lunch, a chicken strips basket with French fries is $4.00. Sandwiches range from $2.00 to $3.00 and the soup of the day is $1.75.

Despite the morning crowd, more customers are served at lunch when specialties such as soup, chicken corn chowder and chicken corn rivel are served.

"The friendly hometown atmosphere makes the restaurant different from others in the area," the owner says, and adds, "It is the people—good and bad—that give me the most pleasure. You learn to know them so well you share with them the good and the bad."

The cafe, neat and clean, has both men and women restrooms, the men's doubling as a storage area which is no barrier to a traveler in need of relief.

Our only regret is that we weren't here for breakfast to be among the farmers and factory workers—and George and Roy.

The Friends Cafe is open from 5:00 a.m. until 1:30 p.m. daily except on Sundays when it is closed.

## NORTH WEBSTER

### COUNTRY KITCHEN
**619 South Main Street**

A narrow porch covers the front of the masonry building which stands alone off the east side of the street.

We have dined here often and the place usually is busy, especially in the summer when Lake Webster attracts boaters, skiers and fishermen.

It's worth a stop if you are in this corner of Kosciusko County.

### NEVA'S PLACE
**720 South Main Street**

Neva's Place is in a strip of stores in a shopping area on the west side of Main, the roof of the frame building topped with a sign that reads "Neva's Place—Breakfast, Lunch, Catering."

Like the Country Kitchen, it is busier in the summer than winter. And it, too, is a good place to have breakfast.

# LEESBURG

## ELLEN'S LUNCH ROOM

### 104 North Main Street

Lunch at Ellen's is like breakfast at other small town diners. Most customers appear to know each other, the result an endless banter among the farmers, other workers and retirees who begin to fill many of the seats at 11:30 a.m.

The restaurant is back off the east side of Main Street in a frame building covered with rough lumber painted a dark rust. The inside is a combination of paint and paneling. There are seats at booths and tables.

A man called Louie, who obviously is a regular customer, sits down at a round table with other locals, and asks Ellen, "What do you have today?"

She responds, "Ribs, country fried steak, hamburger steak, chili, whatever you want." He replies, jokingly, "Got any money?" then orders, "Ribs, or whatever you think I need."

Ellen feigns a moan, "You have to tell them what to order." It is the kind of exchange the customers have learned to expect and would be disappointed without. The customers appear to be farmers or agriculture related employees for this is a small town amid good farm land.

The lunches, including breaded tenderloin and the country fried steak come with mashed potatoes, gravy, the vegetable of the day and bread and butter for $5.50.

Breakfast includes corn beef hash and eggs, $3.50, with potatoes, $4.15. Omelets, half orders, range from $2.50 to $3.60, full orders $3.60 to $5.10. Coffee is 70 cents.

This is a place to enjoy a small town atmosphere while dining in leisure. Ellen's is open from 5 a.m. to 2 p.m. Mondays through Fridays and 5 a.m. to 1 p.m. Saturdays.

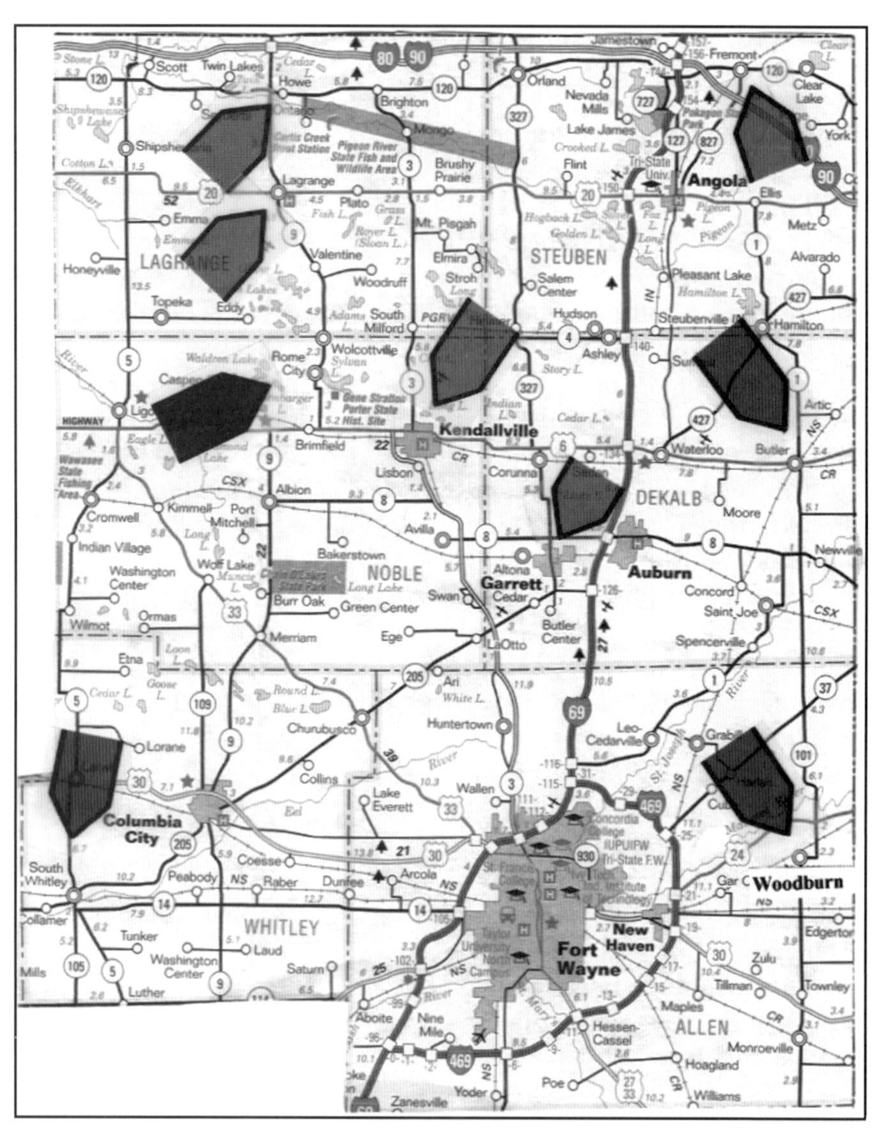


# DINERS — THE FAR NORTHEAST

# THE FAR NORTHEAST

## SOUTH WHITLEY

### THE CORNER CAFE

**202 South State Street**
**(Ind. 5 - main street in town)**

The two-story brick that is home to the Corner Cafe appears to be as old as the town. An awning extends over part of the sidewalk on State Street. Old wood frame windows from an earlier time remain in place.

"Bank" reads a sign over the corner door, but it has been decades since the building housed a financial concern. The Corner Cafe, in the meantime, has become an institution itself.

Inside, the cafe has retained a touch of the past. Antique patterned metal, painted brown, covers the high ceiling. An employee tells us, "We've been told it is copper." Whatever it is, it is a collector's delight and a nostalgic reminder of a bygone time. There are booths and tables, but no counter or stools.

A customer can learn a lot about South Whitley from reading the place mats, the coffee cups and the menu board on a wall. Each contain advertisement for area business.

The extensive menu does not have ads, but it has a drawing of the front of the cafe. And a notation, "If you enjoy your meal, please tell your friends. If not, tell us."

Breakfast, which is served throughout the day, includes choices such as two eggs, potatoes, toast and coffee, for $3.60. The cafe's cinnamon rolls, $1.25, are a tasty treat at breakfast, or at lunch.

The noon special on this day is pork and dressing with mashed potatoes, green beans and fruit, $4.10. For the less famished, a half order is $2.65. The broccoli soup is recommended.

For an extra $1.90 customers can top off lunch with homemade pie á la mode.

The Corner Cafe, owned by Becky Dimmick since 1991, is open from 5 a.m. to 3 p.m. Mondays through Saturdays. It is closed on Sundays.

It is no wonder some local residents come back day after day. “Being friends with my customers (farmers, factory workers, retirees and others) gives me the greatest pleasure,” she says. That and being able to “provide more food for the money.”

The food is good and the employees care about their customers. One couple, arriving later than normal is told, “We’ve been wondering where you were.” The man says, “You know we’ll always get here sooner or later.”

Like that couple, you, too, will likely appreciate the hospitality, enjoy the food and appreciate the atmosphere. Bank on it.

## GARRETT

### MY CORNER CAFE

**121 West King**

As the name indicates, this is a restaurant on a corner. Its windows facing out onto two streets, giving diners a view out, allowing passersby to see what’s going on inside.

Only one customer is inside at 6 a.m. He’s talking with a man who appears to be both the cook and the server.

It is a sharp contrast to Klug’s, a block away. Despite the early hour, pickup trucks line the curb while their drivers have breakfast at the lounge which, at this hour, must be more like a small town diner than a bar.

## KENDALLVILLE

### SHARON’S BREAKFAST HOUSE

**323 South Main Street**

Sharon’s must be a good place for workers and retirees from around this Noble County town to start their days. Cars and small trucks fill the nearby parking spaces at the first hint of dawn.

It's a few blocks from the heart of the business center, but this—for an hour or two—is where the action is. Most of the tables, booths and the five stools at the counter are full at 6:30 a.m. A round table with room for eight is near the front window that faces onto the street.

The diners are a diverse group, mostly men in a variety of occupations. "Butch" is at a table with three other men. He's the owner of Butch's Body Shop, which has one of the ads around the breakfast menu that serves as a place mat. Some of the others also likely are business owners with their own advertisements.

The inside walls of the Breakfast House are covered with grayish colored paneling. Curtains cover the tops of the front windows that face onto Main Street, which give the restaurant an open appearance.

A sign promises home cooked food and the number of diners are an indication that it is as good as it is promoted.

The most expensive breakfast item is $4.50, which includes two eggs, country fried steak, American fries and toast. Two eggs, ham, bacon or sausage, American fries and toast are $3.30. Two pancake turnovers with fruit topping and meat are $4.25.

For the health conscious, grapefruit sections with toast are $2.15. Various other items include mush with bacon, oats, cream of wheat and hot cinnamon rolls.

Saturday morning specials are two eggs, steak and American fries, $4.95, or chipped beef gravy over toast or biscuits, $2.65. Both specials include coffee.

Lunch specials vary. On this day, chicken breast with potato and one side is $4.50. A barbecue bacon and cheese sandwich is $2.95. A half-pound double cheeseburger is just $2.25.

If all those items encourage you to drive to Kendallville, find the 300 block of South Main Street and look for the "Sharon's Breakfast House" notation on the Pepsi sign over the sidewalk.

Sharon's is open from 5 a.m. to 2 p.m. Mondays through Saturdays and from 7 a.m. to 1 p.m. Sundays.

# ROME CITY

## DARI POINT

**Ind. 9 - Kelly Street**

You wouldn't expect to find good food at a place called the Dari Point, but folks around here know better.

The stand-alone masonry building with windows on three sides is busy with breakfast diners at tables, booths and the small counter. A few retirees are among the workers who have chosen to jump start their days here.

Among the breakfast features are the omelets, $2.25 for the three-egg cheese, $3.25 for the three eggs, cheese, tomato, onion, green pepper and mushroom Spanish kind. Most of the men seem to be sticking to bacon and eggs or biscuits and gravy.

The Tuesday lunch special is a grilled "thick" ham steak with potato, side dish and roll for $6.50.

To prove the "Dari Point" in the name, there are both soft and hard ice cream as well as milk shakes, banana splits and sundaes. And it might be well to save room for what the menu promises is "Marge's delicious homemade pie or cake."

Dari Point is open from 5 a.m. to 3 p.m. Sundays through Thursdays and from 5 a.m. to 8 p.m. Fridays and Saturdays. Stop in, if you can, before 8 a.m. and catch the flavor of a small town rising to meet the day.

# LAGRANGE

## MOM'S RESTAURANT

**404 South Detroit Street**
**(Ind. 9 - main north-south street)**

Mom's has been a fixture in this quiet Lagrange County seat since 1948 and it appears it will remain so for years to come.

A menu identifies the restaurant owners as Doug and Tracy Harris, who note, "We work hard to maintain the friendly, family atmosphere and quality home style cooking that has kept customers coming back for 40 years."

It is Election Day 1999 and Indiana cities and town are selecting officials for four-year terms. The interest at Mom's Restaurant is on other matters, however, judging from the conversation of the diners who have filled the small brick diner.

Some of the customers admit they have paid little attention to the campaign that is ending. A few aren't sure who is a candidate for what office.

There are other issues to deal with. Like razzing one of the men who sits alone at a booth. He is a Green Bay fan and his Packers have lost the Monday night television game to Seattle. His jocular friends show him no mercy. His decision to sit alone does not keep them from reliving—to his chagrin—every miserable moment of his team's defeat.

It is apparent this is a place the locals come to start their days with fun and food. And the food is good, the biscuits and gravy among the best we have found on our journeys. A full order is $2.95, a small order, which is still a full meal, is $1.50.

Today's breakfast special is two pieces of French toast with sausage, ham or bacon for $2.75. The omelets vary in price from $2.50 for cheese to $3.75 for Spanish and westerns to $4.00 for one called "The Farmer's." And there is the "Meat Lover's" omelet, which for $4.50 includes ham, bacon and sausage and three eggs.

One of the newer items is called "Mom's Skillet." It is an egg topped with American fried potatoes, sausage gravy and cheese for $2.50. Or for the strong of stomach there is "Mom's Mess," which for $3.45 includes American fries, onion, green pepper, mushroom, Swiss cheese, a choice of sausage or bacon.

Breakfast is served until closing time in the afternoon, but sandwiches, platters and lunch plates are available at mid-day. The lunch special on this Tuesday is cream chicken with biscuit, potato and vegetable for $3.75.

What is called "Dad's Burger" is a quarter pound of beef, shaved ham, two cheeses and grilled onions for $2.50. In contrast, but for the same price, is "Mom's Burger," a quarter pound of ground beef, special sauce, two cheeses, grilled onions and bacon.

A visitor soon gets the idea that the operators have put some thought into their menus, which probably help attract diners. Towns might have better voter turnouts if the polls were at places like Mom's Restaurant. It is open from 5 a.m. to 2 p.m. Mondays through Saturdays and 6 a.m. to 2 p.m. Sundays.

******

We did not stop at two other restaurants north of Mom's on Detroit Street. They are the Courthouse Cafe, 114 N. Detroit, and D. J.'s at 202 S. Detroit. Neither looked as busy as Mom's at the breakfast hour.

# HOWE

## TOWN SQUARE RESTAURANT

**407 Third Street**

**(On Town Square in center of Howe)**

If you are driving through Howe on Ind. 120 look for the sign over the sidewalk on the east side of the square that reads:

**Town Square Restaurant**
**Homemade Bread**
**Pies and Cinnamon Rolls**

Stop when you find it. This is our guarantee you will not regret you did.

It is a place you are almost certain to want to revisit. It is clean, neat, tastefully decorated. "Exceptional," our female companion calls the decor.

And the food, men will agree, is exceptional, especially the freshly-made hot cinnamon rolls, one of which is huge enough to sate the sweet tastes of two customers. The rolls and other home baked pastries are among the reasons why customers from Indiana and nearby Michigan return time and again.

The building is an old, two-story frame next door to the Kingsbury House. Inside a border separates the lower paneling on the walls from the paper above. The floor is carpeted, the ceiling is low, the walls decorated. Another dining room is off to the side.

Many of the tables are occupied at mid-morning on this November day. A group of area residents, five men and one woman, is at a round table. One of the men is wearing an Indiana University cap and a Notre Dame sweat shirt. If he is wearing a Purdue University emblem we do not see it.

Two women in their golden years are at a booth nearby. Couples of a younger age are at other tables. It is a diverse group, where no one seems to feel uncomfortable.

The breakfast, lunch and dinner menus are varied, much more so than at most small town restaurants.

In addition to the hot cinnamon rolls, there are breakfast offerings such as homemade mush with bacon, sausage or ham for $3.95. Two eggs, ham bacon or sausage with hash browns and toast are also $3.95. The cheese omelet with hash browns is $3.50, but the house specialty is a "Farmer's Omelet," which includes ham, cheese, onion, potatoes and bacon for $5.15.

For later in the day, a range of daily specials are available. On Mondays, for example, they include chicken and biscuits, spaghetti with garlic toast or country fried steak plus the soup of the day, which is ham and potato. On Thursdays the choices are beef tips with mushrooms, cabbage rolls, country fried steak with the soups being ham and bean or cream of broccoli.

Owners Tom and Cindy Hackett say it is the "real" homemade foods, mashed potatoes, puddings, pie crust, dressing, bread, the cinnamon rolls and other items that make the restaurant different from others. Those things, plus Cindy Hackett adds, "the personal touch from Tom."

The Hacketts are gratified, they say, "To see the smiles on happy customers faces when they see our huge cinnamon rolls for the first time." A cinnamon roll, which is indeed mammoth, with juice and coffee, is just $3.15.

An added attraction, seen in few other small town restaurants, is the selection of books available for customers to read if they choose.

And, if diners time their visits right they may meet the Hackett's three sons. Cindy Hackett mentions the youngest, born in 1997, "a surprise" for a couple 40 and older. "Every time we have our little guy in the restaurant the new folks always compliment us on our cute grandson. The laughs begin (when they learn differently). He has brought so much joy into our lives. He keeps us young."

She credits Tom for much of the restaurant's success. "A restaurant doesn't allow for a normal family life. Tom is there 60 to 80 hours a week. He makes everyone feel special and lets them know he is grateful they came to our little place."

No matter the selection, no matter the meal, the food will be good, the service prompt, the atmosphere pleasant.

Howe, home to the Howe Military Academy, is just a short distance from the Indiana Toll Road and visitors from Europe and across the United States have taken the exit into Howe to visit the Town Square Restaurant. Chances are most of the visitors recommend to others headed across northern Indiana that they too make the stop.

Cindy Hackett reveals this incident that shows like Howe, the world, too, is a small place: "Some folks headed for Fort Wayne mentioned they were returning from Italy where they had lived for a time. Before the conversation ended, we learned they lived in the same area there as my brother. It turns out their nephew is my brother's best friend in Italy."

In addition to out of state diners, you are likely to see sheriff's deputies, state police, state senators, farmers, factory workers, businessmen and professional men and women at the Town Square.

The restaurant is open from 6 a.m. to 7 p.m. Mondays through Fridays and on Saturdays from 6 a.m. to 11 a.m. when it closes for the weekend.

One more notation from the menus: "Our water is purified through a reverse osmosis system which is used in our food and beverages."

We're not sure what that involves, but it must work. You won't find taste that is better than that at The Town Square Restaurant.

It's a place you won't forget. And one you'll likely return to whenever possible.

## FREMONT

### MID-TOWNCAFE
**3200 West Ind. 120**
**(Toledo Street)**

At mid-morning it is difficult to get a reading on the Mid-Town Cafe. Few customers remain from the early morning crowd. Only one couple from Michigan down for a visit to nearby Pokagon State Park, and a few other diners occupy the booths.

They have a view onto both Toledo and Tilford Streets from the corner building, which has off-street parking. The Mid-Town appears to be as much a stopping place for visitors to the state park and the lake country as for local residents.

"Food so great, you'll scrape your plate," promises a refrigerator magnet. "Try something different for breakfast," advises a sign for a cinnamon raisin bagel.

The breakfast special for this Tuesday is French toast with bacon or sausage for $2.95. The regular Mid-Town breakfast includes two eggs, two pancakes and bacon, sausage or ham.

For the more daring diner there is the "Farmer's Omelet," which includes ham, green peppers, onions, tomato and cheese for $4.50.

The restaurant is open from 6 a.m. to 3 p.m. Mondays through Wednesdays; 6 a.m. to 8 p.m. Thursdays through Saturdays, 7 a.m. to 2:30 p.m. Sundays.

# BUTLER

## BROADWAY CAFE

### 136 South Broadway
### (Ind. 1 through town)

As in all businesses, change is inevitable and it is no different for restaurants. It was in 1996 when we visited Mom's Eaten House at the northwest corner of Broadway and Oak at one of Butler's busiest intersections.

It was a diner decorated with mementos from the past that made conversation for the present. Antique medicine boxes, tools, pictures and programs were on the walls. Old tobacco tins—Velvet, Prince Albert and others—sat on shelves.

It was a delightful place to visit.

On this return visit, the building, a two-story brick, looks familiar. The interior, though, has changed. We aren't sure we are in the right place, until we check the restroom. It is there, we find the Prince Albert tins, anchored in place to foil the sticky fingers of any coveting collectors.

We now know we are in the right place. A friendly waitress confirms that what is now the Broadway Cafe was once Mom's Eaten Haus. The cafe is small, three stools at a counter near a soda fountain and seats at tables for 40 to 50 diners. Pictures have replaced the relics on the paneled walls.

As far as the food and service are concerned, the change in name and decor is of no concern. This remains a pleasant place to visit, a wise stop for those who seek good food in a warm atmosphere.

The breakfast special is two eggs, hash browns, meat, toast and jelly, $2.99. The selections, however, are varied, from oatmeal to hotcakes to omelets.

The luncheon special for $3.95 includes scalloped potatoes and ham, one side dish and bread. A cheeseburger is $2.55. A grilled cheese with a cup of soup is $2.99.

From 2 p.m. to 6:30 p.m. diners can order all the white fish they can eat with a choice of potato and tossed salad for $7.45.

The soda fountain is an added attraction. It is there that $1.00 cherry and vanilla phosphates can be ordered as well as "old-fashioned" banana splits for $3.75 each.

As we noted, nothing stays the same in the restaurant business. Sometimes the new is as good as the old.

The Broadway Cafe in this eastern Dekalb County town is open from 6:30 a.m. to 7 p.m. daily, but closes later on weekends.

## WOODBURN

### BOB'S RESTAURANT

**22031 Main Street**
**(Ind. 101 through town)**

This is a spacious all-purpose restaurant in a small city. It may be called plain old "Bob's," but it's not a plain old restaurant, certainly not your normal small town diner.

It's open for three meals a day, attracting local residents as well as workers and visitors from throughout the area. The camaraderie among customers found in most small town cafes, however, seems to be missing, perhaps because Woodburn is part of metropolitan Fort Wayne.

That doesn't detract from the friendliness of the servers or the pleasant surroundings.

Bob's, surrounded by ample parking, is in a one-story building at the west edge of town on the north side of Ind. 101. Inside the walls are a combination of paneling and paper. Pictures include one of the old nearby Blue Cut Mineral Springs, which, the caption says, "Stands as a monument to what time and neglect can do to man made enterprises."

Breakfast diners are greeted with an extensive menu, including a kids' section, with a "Good Morning, Welcome to Bob's" headline. The "Farmers Special"—yes, there are still farmers in this area near Fort Wayne—is a ham omelet with American fries and toast, $3.75.

The special, corn beef hash, two eggs and toast is $2.95. The regular breakfast special includes two eggs, American fries, meat and toast and coffee for $3.99.

The lunch specials on this day, all $4.50, are chicken, beef and noodles and scalloped ham. Sandwiches range from $1.89 to $3.34. Platters with French fries and cole slaw are $1.95 extra.

Dinner items range upward to $7.95 for a seafood dinner (shrimp, fish and clam strips with potato, vegetable and salad). Dinners are available in smaller portions for 50 cents off the regular price.

The restaurant is open from 6 a.m. to 8 p.m. Mondays through Saturdays and from 10:30 a.m. to 2 p.m. on Sundays.

Pay your bill at Bob's and the cashier is so certain you'll return, she may offer you a menu to take with you.

# EAST BY NORTHEAST

## GASTON

### MILL STREET INN

**200 Main Street**
**(Corner of Main and Mill)**

The Mill Street Inn is not your old-time small town diner in the heart of a business district. It's in a one-level rustic looking frame building set back off Main and Mill with off-street parking.

Like the crushed stone parking area, the all-purpose restaurant, too, is spacious.

A community bulletin board, near the entrance, keeps residents posted on what's happening around town.

Antique implements are on the paneled walls. So are a number of Gaston High School class pictures with individual photos of the graduates. Like in many small towns, the high school is gone. Students from town now attend Wes-Del High, a consolidation south of Gaston.

Gaston, by the way, was not always Gaston. It was, a bit of history on a wall notes, once known as Snagtown. The Snagtown name, it is said, came about when a pioneer settler snagged a pant leg on a stump.

Snagtown became Gaston in 1904 when the discovery of gas beneath the rich soil brought an economic boom to the area. A visitor, noting that bit of history and the memorabilia on display, may get the idea that the Mill Street Inn is a museum as well as a restaurant.

But it is the food that draws most customers. The breakfast menu is extensive, a feature being country style sausage gravy over two buttermilk biscuits for $2.70, a smaller order, $1.60. Omelets with toast range from $3.45 to $4.25.

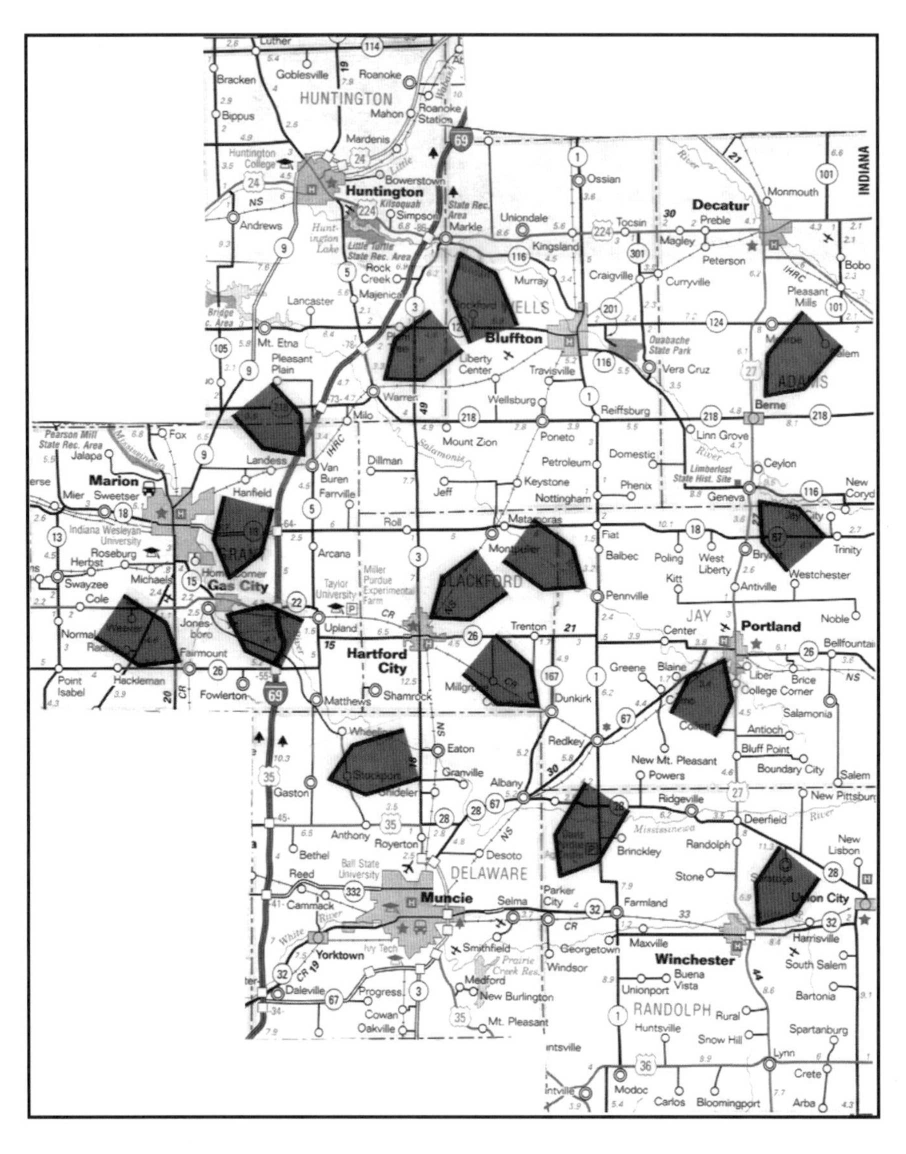


A breakfast of three eggs with bacon, sausage or ham, hash browns, toast and a large glass of juice is $5.50. Grilled tenderloin, with two eggs and toast, is $4.85.

Lunch and dinner menus also have varied selections, from regular sandwiches to Pizza King beef boats, submarines and stromboli sandwiches. Dinner entrees include pasta, Farmer John's chicken, and various meat and fish platters.

Fruit pies are baked in the restaurant and are $1.60 a slice, $2.00 á la mode. Among the other desserts are malts, shakes, floats, banana splits and other ice cream treats.

A small town restaurant with a big time menu, the Mill Street Inn is open from 6 a.m. to 10 p.m. Mondays through Thursdays and 6 a.m. to 11 p.m. Fridays and Saturdays. It is closed Sundays.

## GAS CITY

### JACKIE'S FAMILY RESTAURANT

**105 N. Harrisburg Avenue (Just north of Main Street)**

Jackie's is not a Main Street cafe although it is just north of Main. And it's in a building that stands alone away from older buildings in the heart of the business district. It is, however, a place to sit down, be served and enjoy a breakfast away from fast food outlets.

Pictures, including those of Elvis Presley and John Wayne, are on the walls, which are papered above the four-feet high paneling. The ceiling is vaulted and stools are at a high counter.

It is 9:30 a.m. and the place still is busy with late arrivals for breakfast, which is served until 2 p.m. The menu cover is a drawing of an old-time kitchen range, a coal bucket with shovel at the side, a cat asleep nearby. A mother in an apron is sampling food from a pot.

Breakfast includes the first mention of bologna in 100 restaurants we have visited to date. The bologna comes with two eggs, all for $3.00. A plain three-egg omelet with toast or biscuit is $1.60. The western omelet is $3.75. Waffles are $2.00 each.

A full luncheon menu includes both homemade chicken noodles or beef noodles.

Unlike most restaurants, this one is quiet at mid-morning, the early risers and story tellers having departed for the day to return tomorrow.

A sign in the restaurant could be a reflection of a normal business office. It asks: "Do you want to speak to the man in charge or the woman who knows what is going on?" Almost any male employee anywhere is aware a secretary usually knows more about what is going on than the man in charge.

Merle and Jackie Ingle are the owners of the restaurant which is open from 5 a.m. to 2 p.m. Mondays through Wednesdays, 5 a.m. to 8 p.m. Thursdays and Fridays and 6 a.m. to 2 p.m. Saturdays.

## JONESBORO

### DOT'S DINER

**114 East 4th Street (Just East of Main Street)**

Tucked away on a dead-end street, Dot's Diner is another restaurant that is a bit difficult to find. That hasn't stopped hundreds of people from showing up, though.

Dot's has become a Jonesboro institution, one that is open from 5 a.m. to 9 p.m. Mondays through Thursdays and continuously from 5 a.m. on Fridays through Saturdays.

A collage of individual pictures of customers, 300 or so it appears, is on one wall. "All those have been taken in just two weeks," a waitress explains proudly, indicating the remoteness of the restaurant is not a deterrent to customers.

To find Dot's, look for north-south Main Street, then locate East Fourth. The diner is a half block to the east of Main in an old three-story building coated with what appears to be stucco. Only the word's "Dot's Diner" on the two windows facing the street note its existence. The entrance is through an old wrought iron storm door.

Inside, the walls are painted, the low ceiling covered with acoustical panels, the floor carpeted. There are tables but no booths. Eight stools are at a counter. A photo of the 1934-35 Jonesboro High School Zebra's basketball team is among pictures on the walls.

Other old pictures of Jonesboro were donated to the diner by customers. "They (local residents and visitors) seem to like them," notes Dorothy (Dot) Rennaker, who adds:

"I've been surprised how many customers wanted to be in the montage. Some were even mad because we didn't have their photos in it."

At 8:30 a.m. on this day, most of the tables are occupied. Five people at one of the tables end their planning for a church dinner to say grace when their breakfast is served.

Some senior citizens are critical of their Internet providers, complaining of the time it takes to get a connection. It is another indication of the impact of computers at the turn of a millennium.

The menus are fronted with pictures of what is labeled “the management.” It notes that owners Dot Rennaker heads “the complaint department” that Sherry Iverson is the “financial wizard,” and that Sonny Iverson is “the iceman.”

Dot bought the diner in the mid-1990s after working for Chris Logan, the former owner, for 15 years.

No one takes himself or herself too seriously, it appears, nor is there any pretense to make the diner appear what it is not.

Breakfast draws the diner’s biggest crowds of the day mainly because of the biscuits and gravy and other morning specials. The friendly, family-like, casual atmosphere helps to lure the customers who are farmers, factory workers, truck drivers and retirees.

Biscuits and gravy, “while they last,” the menu notes, are just $1.35, a half order, 65 cents. Omelets range from $1.75 to $4.25. Coffee remains at 50 cents a cup with refills.

The lunch and dinner menus include roast beef Manhattan for $3.00, a shrimp basket, $4.60, or a six ounce “butte” steak, $4.50. Among the sandwiches are a “double hot” cheeseburger, $3.30, or a half-pound grilled tenderloin, $3.35.

If you’d like to see your picture on a wall, stop by Dot’s Diner. You might see it later on the T-shirts the restaurant plans to have decorated with that collage on the wall.

## FAIRMOUNT

### THE LEGEND DINER

**115 South Main**

We were disappointed to locate the address and note that the Memories Diner lives only in memories. The building now houses the Legend Diner, a tribute to hometown legend James Dean, whose likeness appears in drawings on the window.

We are interested in diners that cater to morning customers, so we do not wait for the Legend Diner to open, although it likely is an attraction to Deans’ fans who remain numerous long after the traffic accident that took the youthful actor’s life.

The diner is open from 11 a.m. to 8 p.m. Mondays through Fridays and from noon to 8 p.m. Saturdays.

## HARTFORD CITY

### SONNY'S

**200 East Washington Street**

Do not judge Sonny's restaurant by the size of the crowd at 10 a.m. Return, instead at 6 a.m. and you will note it is much busier.

At mid-morning, only two booths are occupied at Sonny's, which is a block east of the Blackford County Courthouse. The place is quiet enough for a nap.

Only a sign over the sidewalk notes this is "Sonny's." The building looks to have once been used for some other purpose, even though a restaurant has occupied the space for decades. Pine paneling covers the walls, which are decorated with pictures. There are booths and tables, but no stools. The floor is carpeted and fans are on the ceiling.

We order decaffeinated coffee and are told it is instant. We accept the regular grind, percolated, which is good. Our pancake is thin, but heavy, but who is perfect on a Monday morning? We should have ordered, instead, Sonny's "Big Boy Breakfast," which includes three eggs, two strips of bacon, two sausage patties and toast for $2.95.

Also available for breakfast, which is served throughout the day, are two eggs, potatoes, steak, toast or biscuits for $3.95.

The "Big Boy" and other home style breakfasts help make the early hours the busiest time of the day at Sonny's.

We revisit the restaurant the following morning at 6 a.m. It is crowded with retirees, farmers and blue collar workers en route to their jobs. It is apparent this is where a lot of ordinary folks from the Hartford City area begin their days.

"It is," says owner Betty L. Melton, "our customers, their hearty appetites and their compliments that give me my greatest pleasure." That and perhaps seeing her husband, the manager, help with the dishes at the busiest times. Sonny's is open from 5 a.m. to 2 p.m. Mondays through Saturdays.

# VAN BUREN

## MONA'S

### 116 South First Street
### (Ind. 5 through town)

This is a restaurant with a view onto the world, or at least that part of the world that is Van Buren.

Its windows open to the south and east facing the Central Christian Church cater-cornered across the intersection, close enough for Sunday morning diners to hear the music.

Brown and gold awnings are above the windows and the door on the masonry building. Inside, the floor is carpeted and fans turn from their anchors on the low ceiling.

Mona's is open from 5:30 a.m. to 9 p.m. Mondays through Saturdays and from 8 a.m. to 8 p.m. Sundays.

It is mid-afternoon, but several tables are still occupied in the lull between lunch and dinner. Two women are viewing the outdoor autumn scenery from a corner booth. Two other women are watching a soap opera on television, but no one else is paying attention.

"Jim," a senior citizen, is at a table by himself. He reviews his weekend for a waitress, who has asked about his health. He is a regular customer, the kind to which restaurant operators become attached.

We order a slice of chocolate pie and peruse the menu. The pie is excellent. The menu is varied, from breakfast to dinner. Had we been here for breakfast as we had hoped, we would have found the morning diners choosing the "Country Breakfast" or other items.

The "Country Breakfast," and this is country as in farm country, includes two eggs, hash browns or American fries, a choice of two ounces of sausage or ham or two slices of bacon, toast and coffee for $3.99. Omelets range from $3.29 to $4.49.

For lunch, the choices included grilled chicken breast, baked potato and tossed salad for $4.59. Battered fish with French fries, cole slaw and a roll is $4.29.

We finish our pie, and talk with "Jim." He is Jim Gunn, who has stories to tell and experiences to share. Gunn remains a sports fan, having attended each football game the Eastbrook High School Panthers have played in the 1999 season. Eastbrook, he reminds us, is a consolidation of Upland and Van Buren, its athletic teams of the late 1990s having made residents of both towns proud.

Gunn relates humorous stories about his life and his days at Thorntown, another small town southwest across the state in Boone County.

Only in small town diners can you meet men like Jim Gunn, who almost always convert strangers to friends before they leave.

We make a note to return to Van Buren, for breakfast at Mona's and a chance to again talk with Jim Gunn.

## WARREN

### MA AND PA'S KETTLE

**204 North Wayne (Main business street)**

It is almost noon and Ma's serving customers. Pa's back in the kitchen. The "Kettle" is strictly a mom and pop operation. But don't get the idea from the name of the place that this is an older couple.

"Ma" and "Pa" are Rhonda and Greg Andrews and they are younger than most of their customers.

In the heart of Warren's small business district, this is another diner in a building that appears to be as old as the Huntington County town. The restaurant section in the two-story brick is covered in wood painted white as are the bricks.

Inside, the restaurant is narrow, no more than 15 feet wide. The tables and booths are covered, the floor is carpeted, the sides covered in paneling topped with wallpaper. Pictures adorn the walls. The ceiling is high as it is in most buildings that date back a century or more.

The Kettle is open from 6 a.m. to 2 p.m. Mondays through Thursdays, from 6 a.m. to 7 p.m. Fridays and from 7 a.m. to 2 p.m. Saturdays.

Its customers include farmers, factory workers, business and professional men and women and travelers who take the exit off I-69 into town.

It is November and the diner reflects it's the Thanksgiving season. "We try to get into all the holidays with special decorations and seasonal music," Greg Andrews notes, adding, "Ma has a real fun time with customers at Halloween."

Breakfast, served from 6 to 11 a.m., is more varied than that in most small diners. It includes, for example, a fresh fruit bowl, bran muffin and juice for $3.75. A three-egg cheese omelet is $2.75, the Spanish $3.50, the western $3.99.

The ham or sausage "Scram" with toast, coffee or juice is $3.75. The "Farmer's Skillet" includes two scrambled eggs with peppers, onions, sausage, cheddar cheese in a tortilla shell, two biscuits and juice or coffee for $4.50.

Different breakfast specials are available each morning. The lunch specials also differ each day. A different entree is offered on Friday nights, when "all you can eat" fish is on the menu.

Besides the excellent breakfasts and home cooked lunches, the Kettle specialties are homemade tenderloins and apple dumplings with cinnamon topping.

Items on the lunch menu on this Monday include a shrimp basket for $5.29, the chicken and noodles blue plate special, $4.99, or a bacon cheeseburger with a bowl of broccoli soup, $4.99.

No matter what you order for breakfast or lunch you will find "Ma" a gracious hostess and "Pa" a good cook. "Being our own bosses and forming good friendships with customers give us our greatest pleasure," they agree.

Anyone driving on I-69 is advised to take one of the two exits into Warren. The 5 to 10 minutes it takes to reach Ma and Pa's Kettle will be more rewarding than the fast food offerings at intersections.

## MARKLE

### DAVIS FAMILY RESTAURANT

**165 North Clark ( Ind. 5 through town)**

This is a restaurant that could be called the historical center of Markle. It's almost in the center of town and the pictures on its walls show scenes of a Markle of an earlier time.

There are numerous photos of individuals, buildings and pictures dating back to 1910, each having had a role in the history of the town. A notice on a wall notes: "The Markle Historical

Society needs people interested in preserving Markle's history. Membership $5.00."

A couple at a few tables away notices as we view the photographs. They are Mr. and Mrs. Milford Lambert, he, coincidentally, the president of the Markle Historical Society. They are friendly and as interested in other areas of the state as they are in their home town.

But this is about restaurants of today. This one, owned by Robin Phillips, the menu notes, is in a one-story tile building painted brown. Inside, the low ceiling is accented with exposed beams. The walls are paneled and papered. There are enough seats for 75 to 100 diners, who can come here for breakfast, lunch and dinner.

On the breakfast menu is the daily special, called "Best Deal." Served until 11 a.m., it includes two eggs, meat, American fries and coffee for $2.99. The same meal after 11 a.m. is $3.25. A four-ounce sirloin steak, eggs and American fries are $4.65. Omelets with American fries and toast range from $2.60 to $3.95.

The lunch special on this day includes all you can eat chicken with potato and salad bar for $4.75. A Swiss steak with potato and salad bar is $4.45.

Dinner entrees range in price from $4.45 for liver and onions to $6.95 for a Kansas City steak. All items include a potato and the salad bar.

And don't forget the apple dumpling. It's just $1.50.

The Davis Family Restaurant is open from 5:30 a.m. to 9 p.m. Mondays through Fridays, 5:30 a.m. to 2 p.m. Saturdays and from 7 a.m. to 2 p.m. Sundays.

Like Ma and Pa Kettle's in Warren, it is an easy access off I-69. It's a place to start the day with the "Best Deal" and coffee and savor the food while reviewing the town's history.

## BERNE

### PALMER HOUSE

**118 West Main Street (Ind. 218 through Berne)**

There are plenty of good reasons to visit this Swiss community in northern Adams County. The Palmer House is one of them.

A restaurant has been a fixture at Main and Fulton Streets for more than a century, the Palmer House since 1947. It's in a two-story chalet-type structure that obviously has been well maintained, as have other buildings in this town that caters to tourists.

The front of the brick exterior is coated in stucco and painted blue and white. A balcony extends over the sidewalk from the second floor, giving the Palmer House a touch of lavishness not found in most small town diners.

Walls are a combination of paneling and wallpaper accented with paintings and photographs. One is a page from an old magazine with a picture of an Allis Chalmers tractor (circa 1947) promoting contour farming which was used a half century ago to prevent erosion on hilly land.

A front dining room has two horseshoe counters, each with 10 stools, as well as a few booths. Three men at one of the counters are reliving an Indianapolis Colts victory one of them has attended. A dining area to the rear is much larger, its walls decorated with pictures and relics from an earlier time.

This is a restaurant with a varied menu, good food, great service and a pleasant atmosphere. And reasonable prices.

Orders of hotcakes, waffles and French toast are each $2.10. Other breakfast items, available until 11 a.m., also are available. We make a note to return sometime for the Saturday morning breakfast buffet, which is $5.50.

Daily $4.75 lunch specials include beef pot roast, pork steak or chicken. The salad bar is an extra $1.75. The noon menu also includes a bit of philosophy, "Christian hospitality is the bridge between a heart and an open home."

We choose the barley soup. It is excellent, the best we have ever had, a meal in itself without the breaded tenderloin sandwich which comes with it for $3.90.

Dinner entrees, all you can eat of each, include fish on Mondays, chicken on Tuesdays and catfish on Wednesdays. For $7.00 they include the salad bar. The smorgasbord on Friday nights is $8.85.

We recommend a stop—be it morning, noon or evening—at the Palmer House when you are in Berne. Chances are you won't be disappointed.

* * *

The White Cottage Restaurant is nearby at 178 West Main. It appears to be another neat and clean diner specializing in sandwiches and ice cream.

## GENEVA

### HIGH LINE RESTAURANT

**404 East Line Street**
**(Ind. 116 through town)**

If you like covered bridges, this is a place to stop. Pictures of the old spans almost cover one of the walls in this little cafe in the center of town. A collection of Coca Cola, Pepsi and other memorabilia is on an opposite wall.

The High Line is on the ground floor of an old two-story brick coated in light yellow paint near the town post office in the main business block. It is open from 5 a.m. to 4 p.m. Mondays through Fridays and from 5 a.m. to 2 p.m. Saturdays.

We arrive at the restaurant, which has tables but no booths, counter or stools, at a slow time. A lone waitress is wearing a High Line baseball cap. Only one other diner is present, so we do not capture the atmosphere of a busier time. That likely can be done better at breakfast on another day.

Breakfast includes sausage gravy and biscuits, a full order for $3.00. Pancake with bacon or sausage is $3.50, with ham $4.00.

It is 1:30 p.m. but we are not given a menu so we do not learn what has been available for lunch. We do note a sign that says pies are homemade and that the potatoes are "real."

When in Geneva to visit the Gene Stratton Porter Limberlost Historic Site, just a few blocks away, stop at the High Line for your own evaluation.

# EAST CENTRAL

## PENNVILLE

### PENNVILLE RESTAURANT
**195 South Union**
**( Ind. 1 - Town's main street)**

It is mid-afternoon and there appears to be enough residents at the Pennville Restaurant to conduct a town meeting. Men are here, women are here, husbands and wives are here. It may be the second wave of the day, following the breakfast crowd earlier.

This is another diner where everyone seems to know everyone else. "Sara Jane" is back in town from a trip to some distant city. She tells a greeter she couldn't live in "a town like that."

"Kenny" comes in, says he wants a Coke, then walks to the soft drink dispenser, draws some ice and fills up his glass.

Across the way, retirees at a table are sipping afternoon coffee and catching up on any news that has developed in the Jay County town since they were at the restaurant for breakfast. Chances are they may eventually return to 1942 when the Pennville High Bulldogs basketball team won the sectional and the opening game of the regional to be among the Final 32 in the state tournament. And if they are like most small town fans, they may still rue the day when consolidation closed the high school and sent students to Jay County High.

"Many of the same customers are here three to four times a day," say owners Greg and Rita Miller. "It's nice to see the local people come in and visit as long as they wish. They tell us what they want on the menu."

If you are going to relax among friends, this is the place to do it in Pennville. The restaurant in a stand-alone building covered with native stone is neat and clean. Red tile is on the floor, curtains are at the windows atop the Venetian blinds. There are stools at a small counter and seats at tables and booths. A town bulletin board includes a list of antique tractors for sale, some dating back to 1936.

The restaurant is open from 5:30 a.m. to 7 p.m. Mondays through Saturdays and from 7 a.m. to 2 p.m. Sundays. Its clientele includes farmers, factory workers, retirees and Amish, who live in the area.

We regret we are not here for breakfast. A ham steak with eggs, hash browns, home fries and toast is $3.95. Omelets range from $2.35 to $3.45.

Today's luncheon specials were chopped sirloin and ham, beans and cornbread, each with two sides for less than $4.00. "Uncle Bob's" reuben sandwich is $2.99, a double cheeseburger, $2.85.

This, we conclude, is a place to taste the food and flavor of small town Indiana. And occasionally see celebrities, which pleases Greg and Rita Miller. Bill Dance, whose fishing show is seen on cable television TNN, is among those celebrities who have stopped at their restaurant.

## PORTLAND

### KATE'S COFFEE SHOP

**224 South Meridian**

**(One of town's main streets)**

It is seldom owner Ruth Bruss opens the door to Kate's Coffee Shop at 5 a.m. without seeing at least three men outside waiting to enter.

The coffee shop is a home away from home for Portland old-timers. The diner has been a fixture at the same location for 55 years and the city would not be the same without it.

And the owner wouldn't be the same without seeing her customers day after day. "It's the people I enjoy most. That and the fact I like to cook old-fashioned food," Ruth explains.

She took over the restaurant five years ago, retaining the Kate in the name it had been known by since 1944. Kate was Kate Thorn, who with her husband, Charles, operated the restaurant for 50 years.

It is doubtful the Thorns enjoyed the place any more than Ruth Bruss does. She has grown accustomed to hearing the stories spun at what has become known as the big bullcrap table.

"You almost need hip boots to walk through the stuff," she says of the story tellers, most of whom are retirees and farmers.

Ruth Bruss is an entrepreneur who has learned to make a buck however she can. In addition to doing all the cooking, she also bakes pies on order, a one day notice required. Another sign reads, "I sell homemade noodles, $2.25." A notation advises that water is 25 cents for anyone who comes in, asks for a glass but doesn't order food.

And she doesn't waste money on any of those fancy up-town menus. Hers are a combination of hand printing and type, covered with a sketch of a steaming cup of coffee. This is, after all, small town Indiana, not a Ruth's Chris Steakhouse.

Golf balls also are for sale, courtesy of a relative who works at a golf course. "I make a dollar out of those," she says.

But back to that home cooked food, which after all is what draws customers. The breakfast menu is headed "Egg Citement," listing what options are available with eggs. A ham and cheese omelet is $4.39, a western omelet, $4.45. A waffle with ham, bacon or sausage is $3.79.

Customers sometimes jokingly try to order from the souvenir menus from a half century or so ago that remain on one wall. They offer a choice of juice, county ham, two eggs, fried potatoes and coffee for $1.55. Three hot cakes with choice of meat and coffee were $1.25. Two pork chops with potatoes and salad were $1.65.

An even older menu offers a 10-ounce T-bone steak for $1.65 or a half-fried chicken for $1.25.

Times change, prices rise, but little else has changed at Kate's over the years.

Luncheon entrees are homemade meatloaf on Mondays, homemade chicken dumplings on Tuesdays, homemade beef and noodles on Wednesdays, sauerkraut on Thursdays and fish on Fridays. Only breakfast is served on Saturdays when the diner closes at 10 a.m. It is open weekdays from 5 a.m. to 2 p.m.

Kate's is closed on Sundays. An entrepreneur who loves her work needs one day a week off even if she misses the morning crowd at the liar's table which makes owning a place like Kate's Coffee Cup enjoyable.

# DUNKIRK

## CHRISTIE'S FAMILY RESTAURANT

### 126 East Commerce
### (Half block off Main - Ind. 167)

If you are looking for a great cup of coffee, this is the place to stop. The blend is among the best we have sampled.

From the outside, Christie's doesn't look to be a special place. But that's before a visitor notices all the pickup trucks out front or all the retirees walking into the restaurant for breakfast.

The cafe in the long, thin, one-story brick is busy at dawn on a November morning. Men of all ages—farmers, seniors, contractors—have filled a table near the entrance. Seats at a table nearby, too, are filled. A few women and young men pass through the front dining room to one in the back, which is a meeting place for the Dunkirk Kiwanis Club and other groups.

There are booths and seven stools at a high counter in addition to the tables in the front section where the walls are a combination of paneling and wallpaper. The counter front is made of glass squares from an earlier era, indicating this was a restaurant long before it became Christie's (as in owner Kathleen Christie) back in 1993.

Another indicator of the building's age is the old steam radiators which are still emitting warmth on a cool morning.

This is another restaurant where few customers are strangers. A man tells a waitress, "I hope you are in a better mood than yesterday." She laughs to show she is not offended, and replies, "If I was in a bad mood yesterday I'm better today." There is little quiet time in the restaurant at this hour. A visitor needs to be wide awake when he enters to keep pace with the conversation.

But it is food this restaurant is about. "Home cooked food and pies," a sign notes. Another one boasts that the biscuits are homemade.

The menu is imaginative. For breakfast there is the "Two by Four," two eggs, two pancakes, two sausage links and two strips of bacon for $2.99. The "Morning Delight" consists of ham steak, two eggs, hash browns or American fries, toasts and coffee or juice for $4.95.

If one of the farmers up front orders either one, he may not have to come in from the fields until dusk to eat again.

For lunch on this day, the specials are grilled chicken, wild rice and two sides for $3.45. Another option is dried beef gravy on biscuits.

On the dinner menu are such items as a 12-ounce T-bone steak with potato and salad for $5.75. Two pork chops are $5.75. Both can be topped off with pie á la mode.

Christie's is open from 6 a.m. to 7 p.m. Mondays through Fridays, 6 a.m. to 1 p.m. Saturdays and 7 a.m. to 2 p.m. Sundays. And remember a restaurant doesn't need an elegant exterior to serve good food.

## WINCHESTER

### THE COUNTRY KITCHEN

**208 South Main**
**(Block south of Courthouse)**

Take two steps up from the sidewalk into the Country Kitchen and return to the past. This is a diner like almost every town had back in the 1930s and 1940s.

Spend a few minutes with owner Joyce Caylor and you will know that Winchester is fortunate to have a reminder of its heritage that many towns no longer have. The restaurant, which appears to be as old as the town, is in a two-story brick painted light blue, an air conditioning unit extending onto the sidewalk. An apartment above the restaurant is now used for storage.

The inside is small, room for just five tables with four seats each and eight stools at the counter, which faces the grill where eggs are fried to order. It is obvious this has been a busy morning. A one-gallon tin can at the grill is stacked high with broken egg shells.

Coffee is served in an assortment of cups. Ours advertises Rodefeld's Quality Service—Since 1900." A man nearby is drinking from an I.U., for Indiana University, cup.

It is of no matter. People come here to have a good time, tease the owner, enjoy the fellowship and to eat. Joyce Caylor calls her male customers "mean and ornery guys," but she isn't serious when she does. Like most owners of small town diners, it is her customers that make the work enjoyable.

The Country Kitchen is a daily conference room of sorts for its regular diners. "We're like a close knit family," Ms. Caylor explains. "When one of us hurts, we all hurt. We have a good time, even if I have to tame these guys now and then," she says of her male customers. "I should sell tickets for people to listen in," she adds.

Among those males is a barber next door who can hear enough stories over breakfast to regale his customers throughout the day. It is a cast of characters that sometimes includes lawyers, businessmen and farmers. And women, like the one who feels enough at home to walk behind the counter and refill her coffee cup.

Diners agree there has been a restaurant at the location "forever." Joyce Caylor has owned it for 11 years, baking cakes on the side. "You have to do a little bit of everything to survive when you own a small restaurant," she admits.

The Country Kitchen is open from 5 a.m. to 2 p.m. Mondays through Fridays and from 7 a.m. to 2 p.m. Saturdays.

Joyce takes Sundays off. "I have to get away from these ornery guys one day a week," she says, then laughs to let us know they really aren't that bad.

If you're 60 or past, you'll want to stop at the Country Kitchen to recall your youth. If you are younger you may want to see what life was like before McDonald's and Denny's took the personality and merriment out of breakfast.

## PARKER CITY

### PETRO'S COUNTRY KITCHEN

**24 South Main**

**(Near railroad off Ind. 32)**

From the outside the long, narrow building that is home to Petro's Country Kitchen looks new, clean and neat. It has the same appearance inside.

Wallpaper covers the walls above three feet high paneling. Lace curtains are above the Venetian blinds on the windows.

About 60 seats—all at tables—are in the brightly-lighted dining room.

Despite its neat appearance, the building has housed a restaurant for 50 years. It was closed when Eva C. Petro returned to Parker City and reopened the restaurant as Petro's in 1996.

"I have a lot of family here and I was happy to be able to bring my children here to the small friendly community and to revive a nice restaurant," she explained.

It did not take her long to realize how much her customers appreciated having a restaurant in town. "We had an electrical fire shortly after we opened. I arrived after the waitress called me and found the fire department on the scene, the electricity off, but all my customers still at the tables, eating breakfast, unconcerned about the fire. I laughed, despite the fire, when I saw all the people still eating."

It is the customers who make ownership worthwhile. "My greatest pleasure comes when customers tell me they enjoyed their meals and how much they like coming to such a friendly place."

Customers, mostly farmers, represent a cross section of the area's population. The Country Kitchen also is home to the Parker City Lions Club, which meets here on the second and fourth Mondays of each month.

We order biscuits and gravy, which are excellent, the biscuits fresh, the cost $3.00 for a full order, $2.15 for a half order. Pancakes with sausage, bacon or ham are $3.20. Omelets range in price from $2.30 to $3.75.

Smoked pork chops and eggs served with hash browns and toast or steak and eggs with hash browns and toast are $6.05. The $4.75 "Breakfast Bowl" is scrambled eggs topped with onions, sausage, cheese, potatoes and gravy. It is an item to please farmers and others who work hard for long hours.

Breakfast is available throughout the day. "We charge for what you order, not for what you don't want," the owner adds.

Dinner specials for November include T-bone steak for $9.95 or a rib-eye for $5.95. As for lunch and breakfast, the dinner menu choices are extensive. The specials, Mrs. Petro says, include fresh made hamburgers and hand-breaded tenderloins.

For a quiet meal in a pleasant atmosphere this is a place to stop for anyone who plans to be in the Muncie area from 5:30 a.m. to 9 p.m. Mondays through Fridays or from 5:30 a.m. to 2 p.m. Saturdays.

## GREENS FORK

### MISS ETTA'S EATERY

**17 East Pearl**

**(Also Ind. 38 - town's main street)**

If your mate is into antiques and you're not, Miss Etta's is a good place for you to relax. An antique store is across the street from the diner in the town's main business block.

Etta's Eatery is in a frame building that looks like it could have once been a residence. It is in two rooms facing the street, the entrance under a roof on the side. The walls are paneled and papered and the tables are covered with what appears to be oil cloths.

We make our stop at mid-morning when the local residents share a table in the front section. It is the table of choice. Once the seats there are vacated two men, who are in the side room, pick up their food and move there.

Most customers appear to be regulars. One leaves, announcing that he will see those who remain "tomorrow." Coffee cups on the wall indicate they are reserved for the regular diners.

The usual breakfast items are available as are daily luncheon specials, those being country fried steak on Mondays, meatloaf on Tuesdays, pork chops on Wednesdays, fried chicken on Thursdays and deep fried Alaskan fish on Fridays. The $4.75 meals include the vegetable of the day and a choice of tossed salad, cole slaw or apple sauce and a drink.

Chances are, eating here is cheaper than shopping at the antique shops on Ind. 38 through town.

# SPICELAND

## SPICELAND FAMILY RESTAURANT

**6641 South Ind. 3**
**(Spiceland's main thoroughfare)**

This is a restaurant that has diversified. A car wash and walk-up ice cream window are a part of the operation. And visitors can buy lottery tickets if they choose.

Inside the newer brick building the restaurant looks much like a typical Main Street diner. Tables and chairs, all oak, look new. Booths have padded seats. A few pictures are on walls under a low ceiling.

The banter is typical of most small town eateries: "Linda, ain't you gonna tell me bye?" Linda, the server, replies, "Bye, Bobby." Bobby is a senior citizen who likely stops by each day.

The menu offers items for working men and hungry visitors. Two eggs with rib-eye steak are $8.25. Biscuits and gravy are $1.95.

For lunch, the special is pork chops with two sides for $4.45. Pies of the day are Dutch apple, chocolate and sugar cream.

And, a reminder: Be sure to ask for the fried biscuits with apple butter. They may be the best you will find north of Brown County.

The biscuits alone are tasty enough to make a stop worthwhile if you are in the Spiceland area or on your way to tour the Indiana Basketball Hall of Fame up the road in New Castle.

# KNIGHTSTOWN

## KNIGHTSTOWN CAFE

**12 East Main Street, (U.S. 40 through town)**

There are three restaurants in a 3-block span on Main Street, which is U.S. 40 in Knightstown. We ask a local woman for advice.

She recommends the Knightstown Cafe. "It's the busiest, has the best food and the best surroundings," she tells us.

The cafe is on the street level of an old two-story brick on the north side of Main Street, which is U.S. 40, the National Highway.

Cedar shake shingles are on an overhang over the street. Curtains are on the windows onto the street.

Inside, the restaurant, which is no more than 25 feet wide, is nicely decorated with bright Halloween illustrations on a late September day. The floor is carpeted, the high ceiling plastered, the walls painted above wallpaper.

It is a popular place. We count 26 people at seats at mid-morning, women at some tables, men at some others, mixed couples at others.

No matter who they are, be they men, women, retirees, farmers, factory workers or those in professions, all will be given attentive service. "We like our customers," says Sharon Manning, who has owned the restaurant since 1994.

"The fact the restaurant is a very friendly place makes it different from others," she adds.

Breakfast menus include the normal fare, two eggs, bacon or sausage, for example, being $2.85. With ham the cost is $2.95.

Specialties of the Knightstown Cafe are the home cooked food and the jumbo tenderloins. "All you can eat" catfish with two sides are available on Friday nights for $6.95.

Hours for the cafe are 6 a.m. to 7 p.m. six days a week.

If you are looking for a retiree in Knightstown or a worker who needs to start his day with coffee you are likely to find him or her at the Knightstown Cafe.

## MEL'S DINER
### 132 East Main

East on Main Street from the Knightstown cafe is Mel's Diner, which is in a two-story building with a cornice across the top. A roof extends about four feet over the sidewalk.

Marilyn and Melvin Manning started a restaurant at the spacious location in 1995, serving farmers, factory workers, tourists and local businessmen and women. They also cater banquets and provide a meeting place in the restaurant for at least one service club.

Among the diner's specialties are home cooked meals, barbecue, desserts and Mel's chili.

All three meals are served at the restaurant, with lunch the busiest. The hours are 6:30 a.m. to 7 p.m. Mondays through Saturdays.

* * *

A third alternative for breakfast in Knightstown is the Corner Bakery and Coffee Shop at 201 East Main.

## CARTHAGE

### GUS'S CAFE

**8 East Mill Street**

Sometimes the best surprises come inside average looking packages. Gus's Cafe in Carthage, a northeastern Rush County town of 900, is among such surprises.

Few if any small town restaurants are neater and cleaner than this one Brenda and James Magee have owned for almost 20 years.

It looks so-so from the outside, its location, a thin two-story with its brick siding painted gray. A bay window in the front, however, gives a hint that this is not an ordinary store front diner.

Step inside and escape the routine. "Where good friends gather," a sign says. A waitress explains the cafe was redecorated in late 1998. The walls are neatly painted, the tile floor spotless. The booths, tables and chairs still look new. The entire place looks spotless.

And service is good, too. The waitress brings glasses of water without being asked. The menu is extensive, the breakfast selections varied. Two eggs and toast with ham, bacon or sausage are $2.95; a three egg omelet is the same price.

The biscuits are homemade, "We bake everyday, sometimes, two times a day," the waitress brags.

It is a good place for lunch, too. On this day the special is ham and beans, cornbread, mashed or fried potatoes, cucumber and onion salad and spinach for $3.80. The salad bar is $4.25.

Dinner selections are haddock with two sides and bread for $3.95, a ham dinner $3.80 or a three-piece chicken dinner $5.25.

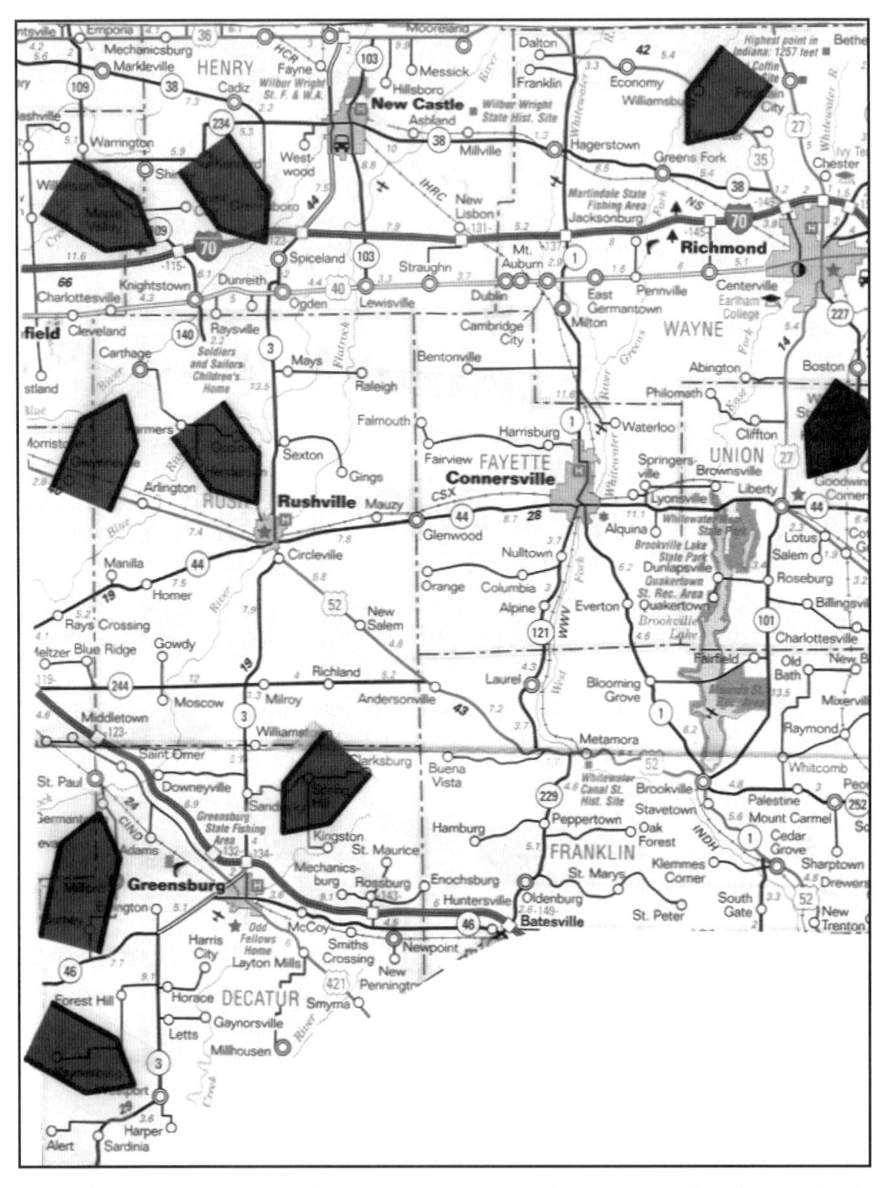


Four men at a table near the kitchen are rehashing their lives as retirees are apt to do, mixing in comments about the farm economy with sports.

A woman alone at another table bids adieu to the men as they leave. Two women are at another table, two couples at another. Like all customers they appreciate the cafe's daily cooked specials and the full service menu.

It is not surprising that Brenda and James Magee have stayed in business for almost two decades.

Gus's Cafe is open from 6 a.m. to 8:30 p.m. daily, except Sundays when it is closed.

# RUSHVILLE

## THE CORNER RESTAURANT
### 250 North Main
### (Ind. 3 through town)

It is 6:30 a.m. and the Corner Restaurant appears to be the social center of Rushville. The place is bustling with chattering customers, mostly men, and new arrivals continue to enter the diner.

It is one of the busiest of 140 diners we will visit throughout the state.

There is nothing elaborate or special about the inside decor, nothing memorable about the decor. But, its diners are not fashion critics. They are here for the food and the fellowship and they give each a four-star rating.

The customers all seem to know each other. "You all right, Frank?" someone asks as a man in bib overalls enters. Frank nods that he is well.

"When I get to his age, I hope I'm as well as he is," a man at the next table declares. Another man complains about his fishing luck. "You know, we've caught 38 bass the last three times we've been out, and not one—not one—was a keeper. That's disgusting."

Another man at the same table, laughs, then tells him, "You wouldn't know a keeper if you saw one."

Another arrival is greeted with, "You win the ugly award for the day." Another customer is welcomed as "Boss Hogg."

"Harold" enters, a two-day growth of whiskers on his wind-weathered face and a Big O Tire cap on his head. He is asked, "How come you are late." He ignores the question and picks up on the conversation instead.

The restaurant is a living community newspaper. The word passes quickly here, the conversation flows freely, covering hard news, gossip, entertainment, sports and maybe a rundown on the day's garage sales.

A waitress asks what must be a regular customer if he wants eggs. He tells her, "You have it down pat. It is egg day for me."

She approaches our table and asks, "Do you know what you want?" Chances are most of her customers already know what is available, but we ask for a menu.

"Home Cooking," the menu promises. It is just 6:30 a.m. but the waitress advises she still has biscuits and gravy. Our companion chooses oatmeal, a full bowl for just 75 cents. We order the biscuits and gravy, passing up other breakfast choices such as steak and eggs for $4.40.

Breakfast is available at any hour even though lunch and dinner are served at the restaurant, which, the menus says, is owned by Virginia Evans.

Sandwiches include the $2.00 "Plowboy," this being a farming center. The most expensive sandwich is $2.50. A T-bone steak at dinner is $8.00, a Delmonico steak, $7.50. Cream pie is $1.50, fruit pie, $1.

The Corner Restaurant is easy to find. It's on Ind. 3 (which is Main Street), one block north of the Courthouse Square. Look for the corner building which appears to be covered in vertical vinyl siding.

## ST. PAUL

### CORNER RESTARAUNT

**117 East Washington (Main business block)**

If it wasn't for the Corner Restaurant name on the Pepsi sign over the sidewalk, you might think you were entering a bank.

Two columns frame the entrance to the stone front of the two-story brick, that, indeed, was once a bank. It also has housed a dental practice.

But those things are in the past. We enter through an alcove and step into the present where nine men are seated at a round table discussing the news of the day.

It is 8:45 a.m. and most of them are drinking coffee from cups with their names on them. They are regulars, whose cups are on the counter when they arrive. Other cups hang from the ceiling.

No one is a stranger here. A lady greets us as we enter, a man does as he walks by our table.

The floor is carpeted. Tables can seat 50 diners, but there are no booths or stools. The kitchen area is off to the side. Walls are papered up four feet, plastered above that. An old bow saw is on one wall. Assorted salt and pepper shakers are on a ledge. Curios, including an iron seat from an old farm implement, are on display.

A sign in the serving window notes that this is "Alice's Place." We soon learn that Alice and Curtis Hicks are the owners of the restaurant which is open from 5:30 a.m. to 2 p.m. daily.

This is down home dining. One of the framed comments on display reads, "If you are grouchy, irritable or just plain mean, there will be a $10 charge just for putting up with you." Chances are there are few $10 fines assessed.

The food? We order oatmeal, which is excellent, no lumps, well done to perfection. The daily breakfast special is "two eggs, taters, toast and coffee, $2.50." For the same price diners may opt for two pancakes, sausage and coffee."

This is a small business. Our waitress steps out while we await our oatmeal. She returns with a gallon of milk. We apologize for making her visit the store. "No problem. Had to go out for others items, anyhow," she says.

We appreciate her effort. The last time we ordered oatmeal at a franchise restaurant we were told we'd have to wait for the milk to thaw.

This is another restaurant where you can "bank" on the food being good.

## GREENSBURG

### STORIE'S RESTAURANT

**109 East Main Street (Across from Courthouse)**

Anyone who drives through Greensburg on U.S. 421 can't miss Storie's Restaurant. It's on the south side of the Decatur County Courthouse, noted for the tree growing from its tower.

Storie's is on the street level of a three-story brick building, its front appearing to be marble. The restaurant, established in 1977, is narrow but deep with scores of seats at tables and booths. Nine stools are at the counter along one side.

We enter the restaurant at 8 a.m. and unlike small town restaurants elsewhere it is women, not men, who have gathered for a gabfest. Eight of them, all senior citizens, are gathered at a table, sipping coffee, too busy talking to order just yet.

We see no men past retirement age. They may gather elsewhere for Storie's seems to be more businesslike than cafes in smaller towns.

This after all is Decatur County's best restaurant, designated so by *The Greensburg News* in 1998, the acclimation on the plaque hanging on a wall near the entrance.

The breakfast menu, featuring advertisements for area businesses, is extensive, the prices reasonable. A western omelet, for example, is $3.50; a full order of biscuits and gravy $2.10.

Diners at lunch and dinner also find a wide selection. A "whole" beef Manhattan, for example, is available for just $3.90.

And the pies, also called the area's best by *The Greensburg News,* are a must. They are, at this early hour, coming from the ovens, and cooling for serving later in the day. Their aromas drift throughout the dining area, luring breakfast diners to return at a later hour.

We make a note of one observation. The waitresses, perhaps because of the early hour, did not appear overly friendly. And they offered coffee refills only to their own customers, bypassing diners who were being served by someone else.

That is a minor irritation. If you are near Greensburg, Storie's is, after all, the best place around to eat. It has a plaque on the wall from the city's daily newspaper to prove it.

## WESTPORT

### YE OLDE DOWNTOWN RESTAURANT

**213 East Main Street**

It is 7 a.m. on a weekday and Ye Old Downtown Restaurant has been open for 90 minutes.

Ten men already are at one table. It is a diverse group, one man is wearing a white shirt and tie, others are in work clothes, some have caps advertising farm suppliers. Two of them read the morning newspaper while the others talk.

They are at what Vickie McDaniel, who owns the restaurant with husband Robert, calls the Liar's Table. "They are coffee drinkers who are a great bunch of people. I love listening to their stories," she says.

Three men and a woman are at another. Four men at a third table are reliving high school basketball games played in small gyms decades ago. Now that class basketball has come to Indiana, the days when every small school hoped to slay the Goliath live only in memories.

We take a seat at another table and wait. The woman diner walks by and explains gently, "You will need to go to the serving ledge, ring the bell and place your order."

This is a one-person operation. We do as suggested and are served within minutes by the cook/server.

The McDaniels took over Ye Olde Downtown in April, 1999, having already owned the building, the lower level of which had housed a diner for at least 35 years.

As in most old buildings, the dining room is narrow and deep. The walls are paneled up to the low ceiling, which is covered in acoustical tile. The walls are bare except for a few pictures and a couple of messages, which indicate philosophy is served here as well as food. One notes, "Skillful listening is the best remedy for loneliness and laryngitis," the other, "Truth is always narrow, but never goes in all directions."

A collection of Beanie Babies, a craze of the late 1990s, is in a display case up front.

The coffee is always freshly-brewed, the cooking like it was back home, the fish, chicken and roast beef specialties tasty, and the friendship enjoyable.

This is not a place for the pretentious. But the coffee drinking teachers, farmers and retirees who gather here each morning like it just fine. They should. It's a slice of Indiana people who stop at fast food outlets or upscale restaurants never see.

## BROOKVILLE

We drive into Brookville on U.S. 52, which is Main Street, at 6 a.m. on a Saturday morning in search of two restaurants listed on our Internet yellow pages directory.

We find neither. We find, instead, the impact of another fast food franchise on small town America. A new McDonald's has taken over the breakfast business, catering to those who are passing through town and attracting local residents who no longer have another option if they choose to leave home to eat.

## LIBERTY

In contrast to Brookville, the town of Liberty is just 17 miles and 25 minutes away. There are no McDonald's, no Hardee's here. There are, however, two privately-owned restaurants open on this Saturday morning. Neither is lacking for customers.

### THE LIBERTY BELL RESTAURANT
**215 South Main Street**

The Liberty Bell is in an ideal location to attract visitors to nearby Whitewater State Park just south of town on Ind. 101, which is Main Street. And on this morning it has drawn a sizable crowd of men en route to work and couples with children who have time to eat out on Saturdays.

Unlike many Main Street diners, this one is in its own building unattached to others. A porch stretches across the front and Venetian blinds cover the windows that face onto the street. Off-street parking is available.

Inside, the well-lighted dining room is spacious, accented with silk flowers and dividers. Seating seems almost limitless.

The menu promises "great food at fair prices." We order biscuits and gravy, our grandson a pancake. Our gravy is too spicy for our taste. The pancake has been burned on top. We do not complain for other diners seem pleased with their servings.

The "Sunrise Special" includes biscuits topped with scrambled eggs, sausage gravy and cheese and home fries for $3.99. For

$2.29 each, diners may order three pancakes, a waffle or French toast. Top sirloin with eggs, toast and coffee is $4.99.

Daily lunch specials are $3.49. The famished and the cholesterol fearless may order the "Monster Burger," which is two eight-ounce patties, four pieces of bacon and three pieces of cheese for $3.99.

This is a restaurant that serves big meals, especially for dinners. A 16-ounce T-bone steak is $11.99, a 12-ounce New York strip, $11.99. The "Hungry Man's" platter includes a chicken strip, 21 pieces of shrimp, sirloin steak, French fries and salad for $12.99.

If all that doesn't sate your appetite, you can order hand dipped ice cream or pie á la mode for $2.11. If you leave here hungry you probably are on a diet.

Summer hours for the Liberty Bell are 6 a.m. to 10 p.m. seven days a week. The restaurant is open from 6 a.m. to 9 p.m. in the winter.

## The LIBERTY RESTAURANT
**7 W. Union Street**
**(Across street from Courthouse)**

While the Liberty Bell a few blocks away has attracted a diverse group, the Liberty Restaurant on the north side of the Union County Courthouse seems to have drawn the local crowd.

This is a more typical small town diner, one that is in a two-story brick where an awning extends over the sidewalk. Angle parking is out front on the street.

The Liberty may not be as fashionable, or as new, as the Liberty Bell, but is of no concern for the men and women who come here morning after morning. It's a place to meet friends, share the news, complain about government and farm prices and spin, and respin, yarns.

The diners have grown accustomed to seats in some of the booths that are tattered and torn. They might be unhappy with change and elegance.

It is apparent this is where the locals gather on Saturdays and weekday mornings for what are billed as "home cooked" meals. Ten men are at a table in the center of the room. Two women at a front booth are greeted by a third woman who complains about her lack of success at a riverboat casino.

Four stools are at a small counter in addition to the booths and tables. A second dining area is off to the side, indicating this may be an even busier spot at noon or when trials are under way in the Courthouse across the street. Pictures on the paneled and textured walls shows scenes from around the area.

Our waitress is busy and has to be asked to refill our coffee, but the food is good.

Breakfast, served until noon, features what the menu calls the Liberty Restaurant's "famous homemade sausage and eggs or hotcakes." Two hotcakes with two eggs are $3.55. Homemade sausage and two eggs are $3.45.

Omelets are cooked to order with a notation, "They take a little longer but are worth the wait." A plain omelet is $2.00, a western omelet or a sausage and cheese, $3.65 each. The "Ladies Mess" is $3.75, but we fail to learn the ingredients.

A three-piece fried chicken dinner with tossed salad and choice of potato is $4.95. A rib-eye steak, cooked to order, is $10.95. "Carl's Special" is a hamburger steak, brown gravy, mushrooms, grilled onion and mozzarella cheese for $5.50.

Hours for the Liberty Restaurant are 5 a.m. to 7:30 p.m. Mondays through Saturdays and 6 a.m. to 1 p.m. on Sundays.

This is a chance to observe small town Indiana, read the ads that ring the menu, listen in on the chatter and relax in down home comfort.

# DOWN BY THE RIVER

## VEVAY

### A. J.'S DINER
### 122 West Main Street

This is not your designer cafe of the new millennium. If you're a sophisticate who insists on formal dining in luxurious surroundings, A. J.'s is not for you.

This is a place for down home dining in an easy atmosphere, rustic and rural, a return to the small town cafe of the early 1950s. And it's open seven days a week.

Two air conditioning units extend out onto the sidewalk at the diner which is in the street level of an old three-story building in the heart of Vevay's business district. Customers enter through doors that appears to be as old as the building.

Magnets are on the refrigerator door. So are pictures of area children under the label "Kid's Country." An old crosscut saw once used to fell trees is painted with a turn-of-the-century scene.

We are in the southern Indiana tobacco country. A twist of the area-grown crop hangs from the crosscut. Smoking still is a habit for many of the residents of the area where tobacco remains an important part of the economy.

The ten-seat community table is usually crowded at the breakfast hour, a place where farmers, timbercutters and other workers congregate to generate enthusiasm for the day ahead. Six four-chair tables increase the seating capacity to 34.

A. J.'s isn't spacious, maybe 16 to 20 feet wide. It extends back to the cash registers and a steam table that isn't in use at breakfast.

A 12-foot ceiling is covered in acoustical tile. The walls are paneled up five feet from the floor. A sign informs guests, "This is not Burger King. You don't get it your way. You take it my way or you don't get the son-of-a-bitch."

The breakfast special, a sign notes is "Eggs and Meat, $3.50." Selections are not limited to the special. Unlike Burger King, diners can get almost any item they choose to begin the day.

Daily specials also are available at lunch at this diner in the heart of the historic Switzerland County town. Anyone looking for a retreat from the hustle and bustle of cities can find a respite in Vevay where they can spend the night at the Ogle House, enjoy the view from river's edge, watch the barges ply the Ohio, walk streets bordered by historic homes and have breakfast at A. J.'s diner.

## MADISON

### HINKLE'S SANDWICH SHOP

**204 West Main Street**

We explain our search for restaurants that reflect an earlier era to a couple on Main Street in Madison. They agree, almost in unison, "Whatever you do, don't miss Hinkle's."

"A Madison institution," they called it.

Indeed it is. There may not be another diner like Hinkle's in Indiana. Or in any other state.

An "H" (for Hinkle's) over "Hamburgers" is on the sign that hangs over the street in front of what some might call a hole in the wall on the lower floor of an old brick building.

Inside, a strip of fly paper hangs from the low ceiling, its prey caught in the sticky trap. Beyond are eleven stools at a counter which fronts the serving area. There are no tables, no other seats, for there is little room in the main dining area which is maybe 20 feet wide and 30 feet long. An old fluorescent light extends over the counter. A juke box sends a country western song bouncing off the walls. A room off the side provides additional seating.

Customers come and go, for there is little wait for food. A young adult is at the grill which faces out on the street, a half dozen or so hamburgers asizzle. He is wearing a rainbow colored shirt, as is the amiable waitress, each noting "Hinkle's Since 1933."

On this day most of the customers seem to be regulars, but the appearance of strangers goes unnoticed for there have been many over the decades, some to savor the hamburgers, others to view a slice of life all but gone from the American scene.

But this is more than a hamburger joint. The breakfast menu is still available at lunch, but for those who prefer lunch the $3.99 special on this day is a white fish sandwich or "Mom's" meatloaf with choices of cottage cheese, slaw, mashed potatoes, green beans, or macaroni, bean or potato salad. The soup of the day is potato, $1.50, served like the plate lunch from a kitchen in an alcove off the dining-grill area.

A curious customer orders a 69-cent cheeseburger. He is not too surprised when it's not much bigger than an oversized silver dollar. He savors the ketchup flavored taste and admits it's a bargain, even a White Castle would appreciate. A hamburger without cheese is 59 cents. There is no extra charge to watch it being fried on the old-time griddle.

Dessert? Sure! Thirty different flavors of "exotic ice cold milkshakes," a sign promises. We try the banana split shake and are not disappointed. This place is a White Castle, plus a Baskin-Robbins.

Owner Jack Le Grand reports the restaurant serves between 500 and 700 customers a day. That translates for a week into 7,000 hamburgers and 600 pounds of home fries, the long-time specialties of Hinkle's.

Le Grand, who has operated the nine-decade old restaurant since 1996, has learned his customers come from all walks of life. They can stop in from 5 a.m. to 10 p.m. Mondays and Tuesdays or anytime from 5 a.m. Wednesdays until 4 a.m. Sundays, the restaurant being open 24 hours a day in the interim.

This is an experience in dining, recommended for anyone except, perhaps, snobs and the sophisticated who prefer to experience the glitter of more prestigious surroundings.

## HAMMOND'S FAMILY RESTAURANT
## 221 East Main Street

Two blocks east on Main from Hinkle's is Hammond's or as a sign out front says, "The Hammond's Family Restaurant—Where Friends Come to Eat."

This is another restaurant on the ground floor of a two-story red brick building in the center of a downtown shopping area that, unlike small towns elsewhere, has maintained businesses in its store fronts.

A canopy is above the only window that faces onto the street.

Fourteen stools line a counter. Nine oil-cloth covered tables that can seat four diners each take up much of the remainder of the narrow dining area. Acoustical tile covers the ceiling, wood panels the walls.

At 7:30 a.m. Hammond's appears to be a man's restaurant. Only two women stop in to dine in an hour's time, even though the men speak softly and say nothing in their conversations to offend female guests.

The men, it appears, prefer to relive World War II, talk about their yesterdays, discuss speed races on tracks or on rivers like the Ohio nearby, argue about sports or talk about the latest developments in this historic city. A TV is on in the corner, just in case there is a sports scene the crowd wants to view.

This, too, is a Madison landmark, a place for Indiana University basketball and NASCAR fans to exchange opinions. I.U. calendars with team pictures dating back a decade or more are on the walls. So, too, are autographed pictures of NASCAR drivers. But it is Dale Earnhardt, who gets the most attention. The aisle between the counter and the tables is called Earnhardt Drive and leads back to a section labeled the Earnhardt Room.

A menu is on the wall facing the counter. The breakfast choices are topped by a choice of two eggs, bacon, ham or sausage and toast for $2.50, a price that brings no complaints.

Coffee is served in a variety of cups that appear to have been collected from various sources or left by customers. Ours is labeled "Racing Daily Form - America's Top Authority." It is appropriate for a place with a sports decor.

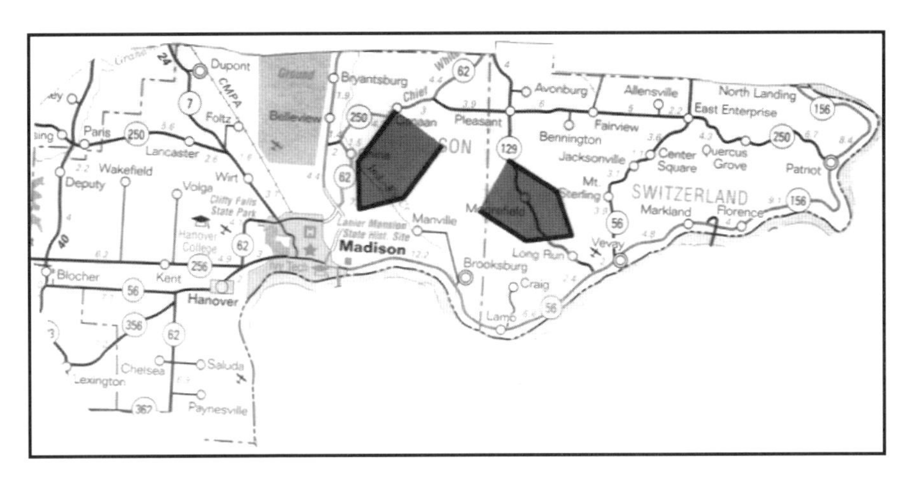


The cups are conversation pieces, as if any additional topics are needed. They are filled by a waitress, or the man behind the counter, without a request for this is a friendly full-service stop, far from the fast food establishments high on the hill and away from the river.

And beware. This is not a stop for fault finders or complainers. A sign behind the counter warns: "If you are grumpy or just plain mean, there will be a $10 charge just to deal with you."

It is, however, a warning that should not be taken too seriously.

## THE MAIN CAFE
## 313 East Main Street

Another Main Street restaurant in the Ohio River City is the Main Cafe, across the street from the Jefferson County Courthouse. It, too, is on the street level of another old two-story brick.

"No public restroom," a sign out front proclaims. It's probably there to deter visitors who come to this 200-year-old city to view the river, look at the historic buildings and attend annual events, such as the Madison Regatta, that bring huge crowds to downtown Madison.

A "Help Wanted" sign is outside, but the one waitress and cook are sufficient to serve the few customers at breakfast at 8 a.m.

Two fans cool the air as does an air conditioning unit in a transom over an opening between the dining area and the kitchen. The cafe, its walls paneled in wood, its floor covered with inlaid tile, is small. Ten stools are at the counter. Three four-seat tables line the center, separating the counter from three two-seat tables that line the opposite wall.

The decor is old, as is the building. A poster for the movie *Casablanca* is near the front. A sign promoting Pinch Hit Tobacco is endorsed by Babe Ruth. Faces of Harry Truman, Robert E. Lee and other names from America's past are on the walls. Another sign is partisan, reading, "Proud to be an Indiana Democrat." Outdated spring sports schedules for three area high schools—Madison, Shawe and Southwestern—are on the place mats.

Smoking is allowed and a waitress lights a cigarette as she talks with a lone woman customer after serving one of two occupied tables.

Breakfast is served at any time, a sign notes. Prices are competitive with the two other diners to the west on Main Street.

And, yes, there is a restroom for customers. For non-customers, there is a $1 fee to use it.

* * *

For those who prefer more stylish breakfasts and lunches when in Madison, the Café Camille is recommended. The popular restaurant at 119 East Main Street offers good food in a pleasant atmosphere and is open at 6 a.m. seven days a week.

Owners Tom and Toni Galassi have seen to it that no one will leave disappointed with the food or service.

# DUE SOUTH

## STINESVILLE

### THE QUARRY DINER
**Heart of Stinesville**

Step inside the Quarry Diner and you know right off you are in a small cafe that is different from most others in Southern Indiana.

Instead of the country music you might expect to hear, it is National Public Radio's *All Things Considered*, which is giving its low-key version of the news of the day. One of three diners at 7:30 a.m. is reading a book about mystics instead of the morning newspaper. No one is smoking, which, too, is unusual.

Tables are covered, then topped with clear plastic. Live plants are in the corners, silk flowers on tables. The concrete floor is painted, the walls plastered and decorated with pictures by local artists.

A piano that doesn't appear to be used often is on a small stage in a corner of the small dining room, which has 24 seats at tables. There are no counter, no booths. The kitchen is off to the side.

The Quarry in the name is part of Stinesville's history. The first limestone quarry in southern Indiana was opened near here, creating the limestone industry which became the area's economic rock. Before consolidation, the Stinesville High School basketball teams were the Quarry Lads.

An historic block, its building made of limestone, is across the street from the Quarry Diner.

The hours for the restaurant depend on the day, so it's best to check before making the trip. It is, however, open by 6 a.m. on

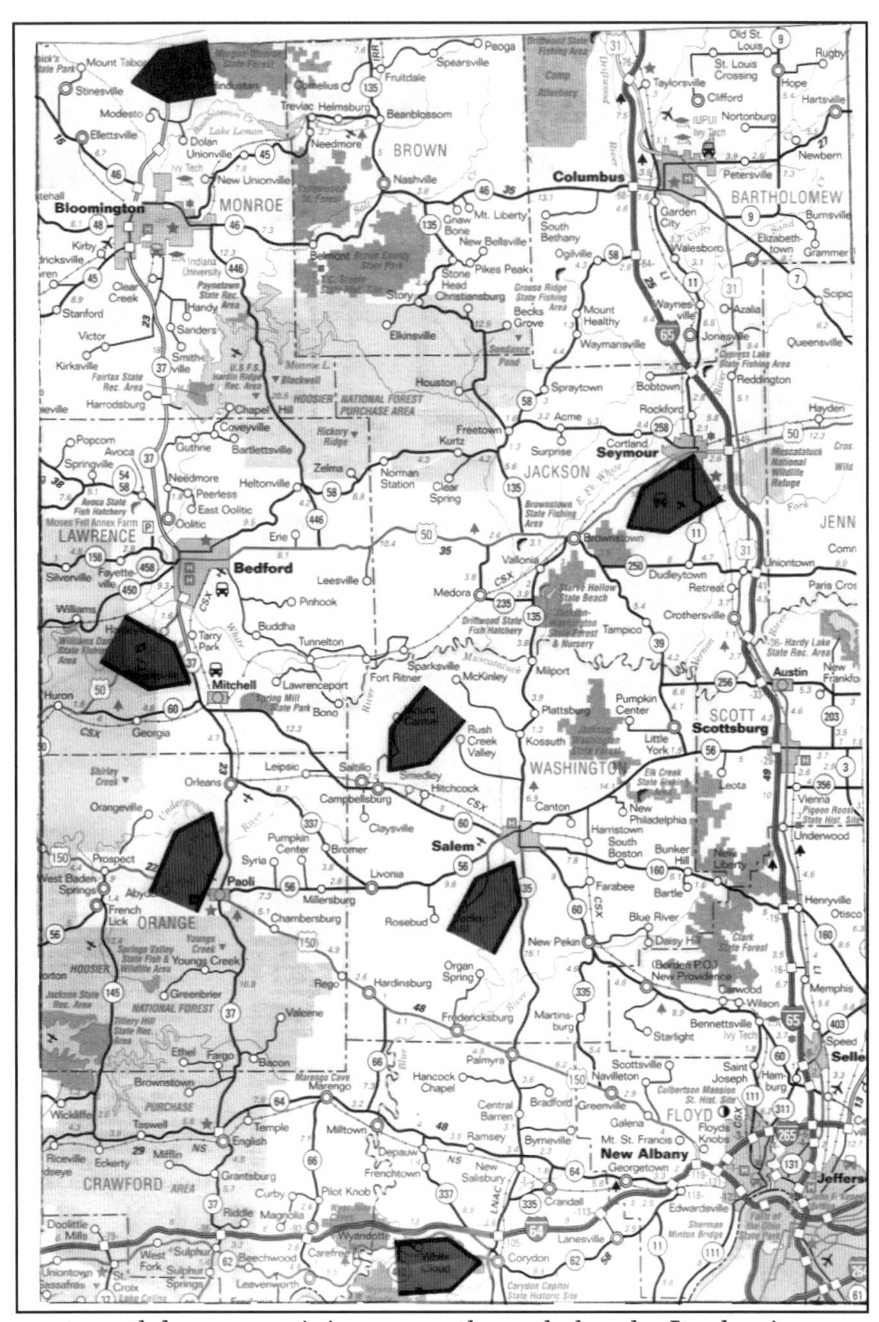


most weekdays, remaining open through lunch. It also is open most evenings.

The menu promises, "Home cooked meals, divine desserts, old-fashioned sundaes, sodas and floats, friendly service." The desserts are well-promoted. A sign reads, "Ask server for great desserts, all fresh and homemade from scratch—you won't regret it."

For breakfast, diners may select items such as two eggs, ham steak and toast, which is $4.99. Biscuits and gravy are $2.00. The "Cowboy Breakfast" ($5.99) includes two eggs, one pancake, sausage, toast or half order of biscuits and gravy. The omelet of the day is $4.50.

This is, indeed, a place of surprises. The coffee is flavored, more like gourmet than the regular grind at most diners. We are surprised again. Quiche, the turkey and bacon kind, is on the menu, not a fare farmers and factory workers in most towns might order.

The server brings us the morning paper, without being asked.

We are pleased, with the service and with the food. The oatmeal, excellent, is $3.35 with toast and that gourmet coffee.

This is a upscale diner in a small town. To find Stinesville go west from Bloomington on Ind. 46, pass through Ellettsville, then turn north on a Monroe County road at the Stinesville sign.

## BROWNSTOWN

### BROCK'S RESTAURANT

**109 North Main Street**

Old-timers say a restaurant has occupied the one-story brick building just north of Jackson County's Courthouse Square for more than a century.

One tells us the diner was there when his father was born in 1896. "It was probably there before that," he adds running down the lineage of former owners. "Roy Brooks' mom and dad owned it when it was known as Brooks'. A man named Bowman owned it, then Bob Coffman bought it before Roy Brooks took it over. It became Brock's when Charlie Brock bought it in the 1960s. Charlie owned it before selling it to Tom and Gail Gray who own it now.

"Charlie Brock's wife still bakes the pies that are sold there," he adds, which may be one reason the restaurant is still known as Brock's.

It remains a small town diner, one to which the locals remain loyal despite the new McDonald's up the street. The restaurant opens each day at 5 a.m. and remains open until 8 p.m. except on Sundays when it closes earlier.

Brock's is a southern Indiana institution, a place for locals to gather and for passersby on U.S. 50 (which is Main Street) to stop for a meal as they head east or west. Ask ten people from anywhere in the area and nine of them likely will tell you they've eaten at Brock's.

"Welcome to Brock's Family Restaurant," the menu says, promising "home cooked meals and homemade pies." Few diners will be dissatisfied, whatever they choose to eat.

Two additional dining rooms, one used at times for meetings of the Brownstown Exchange Club, adjoin the room off the entrance, so seating is seldom a problem. Six stools are at a counter in the room at the main entrance.

Many of the tables are occupied at 8 a.m. on a Saturday morning in September when the annual Watermelon Festival is underway. The waitress is busy, the service perhaps a bit slower than normal, but no one seems to complain even if the oatmeal appears to have been heated in a microwave instead of being cooked from scratch.

Had we been hungrier we would have ordered the meat and cheese omelet for $2.95 or chosen the two eggs and bacon for $2.85.

No matter. It is hard to be too critical of a business that has been a fixture for a century. Besides, we plan to return on a Friday night for the lasagna, tossed salad and garlic bread which is only $3.95. We may return a third time to order the $5.50 seafood platter.

## MITCHELL

### OLD MILL CAFE

**641 West Main Street**

Visitors know they are near Spring Mill when they visit the Old Mill Cafe in Mitchell. A picture of the water-powered mill at the nearby state park is on the window in the restaurant.

The cafe, a gathering spot for area residents, is busy at 9 a.m. on a Saturday. More than twenty customers are in the main dining room. Men at one table are talking about their gambling experiences on riverboat casinos. Younger couples are planning their days. Older couples who have known one another over a lifetime are in conversation.

This is not a hole-in-the-wall restaurant despite its location in an old two-story brick building in the center of the Mitchell's business district. It has the bright look of neatness, its brightness adding to its cheeriness. Walls, painted a light yellow, are lined by pictures that appear to be the work of local artists. Tables—there are no booths—are covered in blue and white oil cloths. The floor is carpeted.

Six stools are at a counter and 36 other seats are in the front cafe. A dining room off to the side, which appears to have its original wood floors, can seat 52 more diners.

The cafe attracts business men and women, factory workers, farmers and tourists for breakfast and for lunch. The hours are 5:30 a.m. to 1 p.m. Mondays through Fridays and 7 a.m. to 3 p.m. Saturdays and Sundays.

The address has been a place to stop for food for decades, being opened more than 60 years ago by the original owner, Bill Cargas, a native of Greece. Another owner ran it for 18 years before Terry Malcheski Lamberth bought it in early 1999.

"We've tried to retain the look and atmosphere of the original cafe," she explains. "We restored the original soda bar and have kept sections of the original tin ceiling. The original walk-in cooler has been repaired and is in use."

Prices are typical of small town diners. An order of two eggs, ham or sausage, home fries or grits and toast is $3.00. Biscuits and gravy are $2.00, pancakes $1.00 each, French toast with bacon, ham or sausage is $3.25. Five choices of omelets are available, the cheddar cheese, $2.50; the ham or sausage and cheese, $3.50; the Loraine (bacon, onion and Swiss cheese), $3.50; the Barcelona (potato, bacon and cheddar cheese, $3.50), and the western (ham, bacon, sausage, cheddar cheese, onion, bell pepper with salsa on the side), $3.75.

Plate lunches are available at lunch when a club sandwich is $3.25, a grilled reuben, $3.00. Desserts are available as is a complete fountain service.

Ms. Lamberth calls the plate lunches, the homemade pies and the soda fountain service the specialties of the restaurant. "We do not serve alcohol, steaks or seafood, so our cafe is different from most other restaurants in the area. Since we restored the building, many townspeople have come by to reminisce about eating or working here, or having lived in the upstairs apartment. Mr. Cargas' daughter still lives in town and visits here often."

This is a small town cafe where no one takes him or herself too seriously. Terry Lamberth, who now lives in that upstairs apartment, tells about the time her dog, Bingo, freed himself and made his way down to the cafe. "The whole place erupted in laughter," she recalls.

We are at the cafe on the final weekend of the town's annual Persimmon Festival. It's an event that explains a sign in the restaurant, "Whole Persimmon Pudding, $10."

Anyone wanting something to do on an autumn weekend should consider Spring Mill State Park, the Persimmon Festival and a stop at the Old Mill Cafe. And, perhaps, pick up a persimmon pudding, which isn't available at many other restaurants.

## ORLEANS

### MARSHA'S UPTOWN CAFE

**156 South Maple Street**
**(Ind. 37 through Orleans)**

Okay, okay! So the sign out front still says, "Herle's - Maple Street - Since 1916." And the name on the maroon-colored awning across the front reads, "Herle's."

After all, it is hard to erase history. Herle's is now Marsha's Uptown Cafe, but the tradition for good food in a pleasant setting continues at the address which has been a restaurant for 90 years.

Marsha is Marsha Higdon, the owner since the mid-1990s who has maintained some of the features of the past while adding to the cafe's attractions.

We arrive at 8:20 a.m. on a Saturday and most of tables and booths are occupied. The diners represent a cross section of people from the area. There is "Menlo," whom everyone seems to know, and there are senior citizens, a young couple, a father and son.

Up front, a large mirror that appears to once have been in a bar, is against the wall. It now is used as part of a soda fountain. It is something that has been here "forever," something that will remain, we are told.

The diner appears to have been newly-decorated to reflect Marsha's personality. It appears brighter, more cheerful. Black and white tile blocks cover the floor. A strip of wallpaper depicting rural scenes divides the walls at the three-foot level. Pictures, dried flowers and baskets decorate the walls.

Booths, uncluttered like those at a Cracker Barrel or some other chain restaurants, are clear. That's because each booth has a shelf on the wall to hold a roll of paper napkins, salt and pepper dispensers and small baskets that contain jellies.

"The very clean, country atmosphere," Marsha says, "is what makes the restaurant different from others in the area." That and the home plate lunches, she could have added.

Marsha's Uptown Cafe is open from 4:30 a.m. to 3 p.m. daily. Its breakfast includes the usual fare. Two eggs and a half order of biscuits and gravy, for example, are $3.25. Three pancakes are $2.50.

Those plate lunches are available later in the day as are various sandwiches, a chicken tenders plate, shrimp or pork chops for $6.95.

The Herle heritage continues but Marsha Higdon has added to it. Anyone traveling through town on Ind. 37 is advised to stop to enjoy the atmosphere and to savor the food.

If Marsha's around, she might tell you about the ghost which is said to live upstairs over the restaurant.

## CAMPBELLSBURG

### TILLIE'S C-BURG CAFE

**29 South Sycamore**
**(One of town's main streets)**

Tillie's C-Burg Cafe may be one of Washington County's best kept secrets. It's a diner motorists who skirt Campbellsburg on Ind. 60 may miss if they don't see the roadside advertisements.

To find the restaurant turn north at the blinker light on Ind. 60, drive into town and look for the Tillie's C-Burg Cafe sign on the window.

It is not a big cafe, the seating capacity just 44. There are no stools, no counter. Ruffled curtains are atop the two windows that face onto Sycamore Street. The ceiling is plastered, the walls painted, the floor covered in tile. Pink place mats are on the tables. Menus, covered in plastic, note on the front that Tillie also does catering and that carry out service is available.

A schedule for the West Washington High School Senators athletic teams is on a wall. A bulletin board up front keeps visitors posted on coming events throughout the area.

Tillie's may be a small cafe, but it has a big menu. One breakfast special is the $4.97 "Country Boy," two eggs, a choice of meat, potatoes and a half order of biscuits and gravy. The "Country Girl" for $2.99 includes two eggs, choice of meat, French toast or pancakes. Diners also may order tenderloin with two eggs for $3.50 or steak with two eggs for $3.75.

Omelets are available as are a variety of breakfast sandwiches. So are biscuits and gravy, a full order $2.45. For $3.00, customers can choose a full order with two eggs.

A daily luncheon buffet, which includes the salad bar, is $4.75. Sandwiches range in price up to $3.95 for the double bacon cheeseburger.

Friday night specials are available as is a Sunday dinner buffet. The cafe is open from 5 a.m. to 4 p.m. and again from 5 p.m. to 9 p.m. seven days a week.

Tillie is Tillie Mollet, who isn't bothered by the size of her cafe. "We may not be a large place, but we try to be polite and fast with our service," she say, taking pride in her home cooked meals that are "made from fresh food, not from a box."

Our stop at Tillie's is at 7:30 a.m. on a Saturday. Tillie, herself, is our waitress. She is pleasant and unhurried despite the arrival of other guests. A group of farmers seated at the front community table, are finishing breakfast. It is late September in one of Indiana's driest seasons in years. They are talking about the harvest and the fire danger from the drought.

They greet a new arrival, asking him about his health. He replies, "It's hell to get old, but it beats the alternative."

Six young adults—male and female—arrive to hear his comment. They, too, in years to come will appreciate his words.

And they likely will appreciate the breakfasts they order, which will be prepared and served by Tillie herself.

## SALEM

### DINNER BELL
**305 South Main**

Enter this little cafe three blocks south of the Washington County Courthouse in Salem and the first thing you may see is this notation:

"If we don't take care of our customers, someone else will."

That attention to the clientele has kept owners Jesse and Lois Powell in business at the Dinner Bell for more than 25 years. Lois, though, has been at the diner longer than that, having started to work here on March 4, 1958.

"It has been my life for 41 years," she says in late 1999.

A restaurant has been in the small one-story brick a lot longer, back to at least 1930, maybe longer. Chances are it hasn't changed much in the years since.

It is a reminder of the past; small, narrow and cramped with just enough stools and tables to seat 27 diners. The grill is behind the counter and almost everything is in view in the room that has enough Coca Cola items to make a collector envious. A person could start a Coke memorabilia shop with all the old bottles, trays, pictures, cases and other items.

Jesse Powell downplays the significance of the collection. "We just started having them here ten years or so ago. We had some empty shelf space so we brought some of the items from home. Our customers saw them and started bringing in their own collections."

It was a hobby that has grown into an attention getter, as if a business in operation much of a century needed more attention.

Besides that, it is a fun place, at least in early morning. The radio is playing country music and a singer is moaning the song, "All My Ex's are in Texas." A jokester asks, "Where are yours, Carl?" referring to any "ex's" he may have. The question is barely finished when Carl retorts quickly, "I could care less." The laughter that follows erases any Monday morning gloom.

Carl's detractor isn't finished. As he prepares to leave, he tells Carl, "Have an aggravating day." If Carl minds he doesn't show it. It may be a routine he hears every day from the farmers and factory worker who stop for coffee and breakfast.

Mrs. Powell has taken care of early morning customers and works on the crossword puzzle while resting a spell. Jesse remains behind the counter.

Our pancakes are thin, more like crepes than the fat, sometimes doughy kind served at bigger restaurants. But they are good and there is none of the syrup that comes in a tiny bottle or plastic container. Ours comes in a big jar so it is not necessary to ask for more.

This is more of a breakfast gathering spot for men than women. The men come for coffee, eggs from the grill and to share their lives, their stories and their jokes day after day.

More business is done at noon when the home cooked dinners and 60-cent hamburgers are available. More about the hamburgers later.

The dinners start from scratch, Lois explains, adding, "We do everything, peel the potatoes, cook the beans." And she could add, "And serve the meals."

The lunches vary by the day. Monday's specials are meatloaf or smoke sausage and gravy; Tuesday's fried chicken or beef and noodles; Wednesday's cube steak and gravy or liver and onions; Thursday's turkey and dressing and kraut and wieners; Friday's pork chop and dressing, fish or salmon patty, and Saturday's Salisbury steak or chicken and dumplings. The plate lunches, just $3.00, also include two vegetables, one salad and bread.

Back to those 60 cent hamburgers: They are made with fresh ground beef bought daily. "We use an ice cream dipper for those, which we sell bunches of," Mrs. Powell explains. After 41 years at the place she knows what keeps customers returning again and again.

And if anyone ever gets out of line she can always do what the wife of a previous owner did when pestered. "She pasted the guy on the side of the head with a raw egg," Mrs. Powell recalls.

Chances are you won't see anything like that at the Dinner Bell now, but you can see a slice of Americana that has almost faded into history.

Stop by anytime from 5:30 a.m. to 3 p.m. The Coca Cola collection will be on display and owners Jesse and Lois Powell will be there to greet you.

## MAIN STREET CAFE
### 105 South Main Street

This is a restaurant with a reflection of the 1950s. "Billy's and Dawn's are spelled out in red neon lights against a back wall. So is an I.U. (for Indiana University) sign near the front.

Large pictures of film idols James Dean and Marilyn Monroe are on display in the well-lighted diner, which is just a half block from the Washington County Courthouse. It's two steps up from the sidewalk in one section of the lower floor of an old two-story brick.

Inside, the walls are painted mauve at the bottoms and tops with bright flowered wallpaper in between. Six stools are at a high counter and 45 other seats are at tables in the diner owned by Billy I. Thompson, who claims the best breakfasts in town are served at the cafe.

Nine men are at a big table, reviewing their weekends on this Monday before heading for work. When one departs, another man arrives to take his place and renew the conversation. A retired couple is at another table, perusing the morning paper. The morning news is on a television set, but no one pays attention.

The usual breakfast items are available. The omelets are $3.50 for a ham and cheese or a western. Biscuits and gravy are available with a half biscuit, a full biscuit or two biscuits.

A luncheon special on this day is a pork steak with lima beans, mashed potatoes and a roll for $3.50.

The restaurant is open daily, except holidays, from 5 a.m. to 2 p.m. "And each day," Billy Thompson says, "is a fun day, one in which old friends are seen and new ones are made."

## CORYDON

### JOCK'S LUNCH

**100 East Chestnut Street**
**(At Corner of Capitol and Chestnut)**

The name is Jock's Lunch, but it's a great place to have breakfast as well. Has been since 1949.

"Celebrating 50 Years," a big banner out front proclaims. By the size—and the cheerfulness—of the breakfast crowd it may be here another half century. From Mondays through Saturdays it is a community center, a place where the locals come to start their days among lifelong friends.

Jock's is a fixture on the northeast corner of Capital and Chestnut, the historic town's two main streets which intersect a couple blocks south of the state's first capitol, one of the area's tourist attractions.

The restaurant is in a two-story brick that, like other structures nearby, has been well-maintained. The entrance is neat and attractive, a fitting introduction to the dining room inside.

Jock's is open from 5 a.m. to 3 p.m. Mondays through Thursdays; from 5 a.m. to 6 p.m. on Fridays, and from 5 a.m. to 4 p.m. on Saturdays.

It isn't spacious, three four-seat booths, two round tables that seat six each, maybe another table or two. Ten seats are at a counter facing the grill where bacon is asizzle and eggs are frying.

At 7:30 a.m. almost every seat in the place is taken, one of the big tables is filled with men in seed corn caps next to men in suits, this being another small town where status or station in life is no barrier to friendship. Both men and women are at the booths.

It is a place where no one is overlooked. One diner looks over at another and greets him, "Hey, Rob, I didn't see you come in." If a regular visitor doesn't show up, everyone else is concerned about his, or her, welfare.

"Every community has a meeting place and for Corydon Jock's is it," says Indiana First Lady Judy O'Bannon, wife of Governor Frank O'Bannon. The O'Bannons' permanent home is in Corydon and they are well aware of the restaurant's history. Mrs. O'Bannon explains:

"Jock's has for years been the place where folks come to get the pulse of the city and scent the odor of fried onions all at the same time. When one walks into Jock's on any given day, he or she will run into folks who by their nature reflect what Corydon is all about. You can, in a few minutes, learn what is important to those folks, the news of the day, who's feeling well and who isn't, and the general buzz. It's great."

She could have added that the prices are reasonable. Three hotcakes are $2.00, two eggs with ham, bacon or sausage and toast is $2.50. It's the same for sandwiches at noon. A breaded pork tenderloin is $2.50; the barbecue mesquite $2.00; the chicken strips, $2.65, and a cheeseburger 80 cents. An item called the "Garlic Pepper Turkey Burger" is $1.50.

You can come to Corydon for at least two reasons. One is a refresher course on Indiana history, the other to stop at Jock's. You will not be disappointed with what you find in either.

And you might even run into Indiana's First Couple, Frank and Judy O'Bannon, if they are back home in Corydon for a weekend.

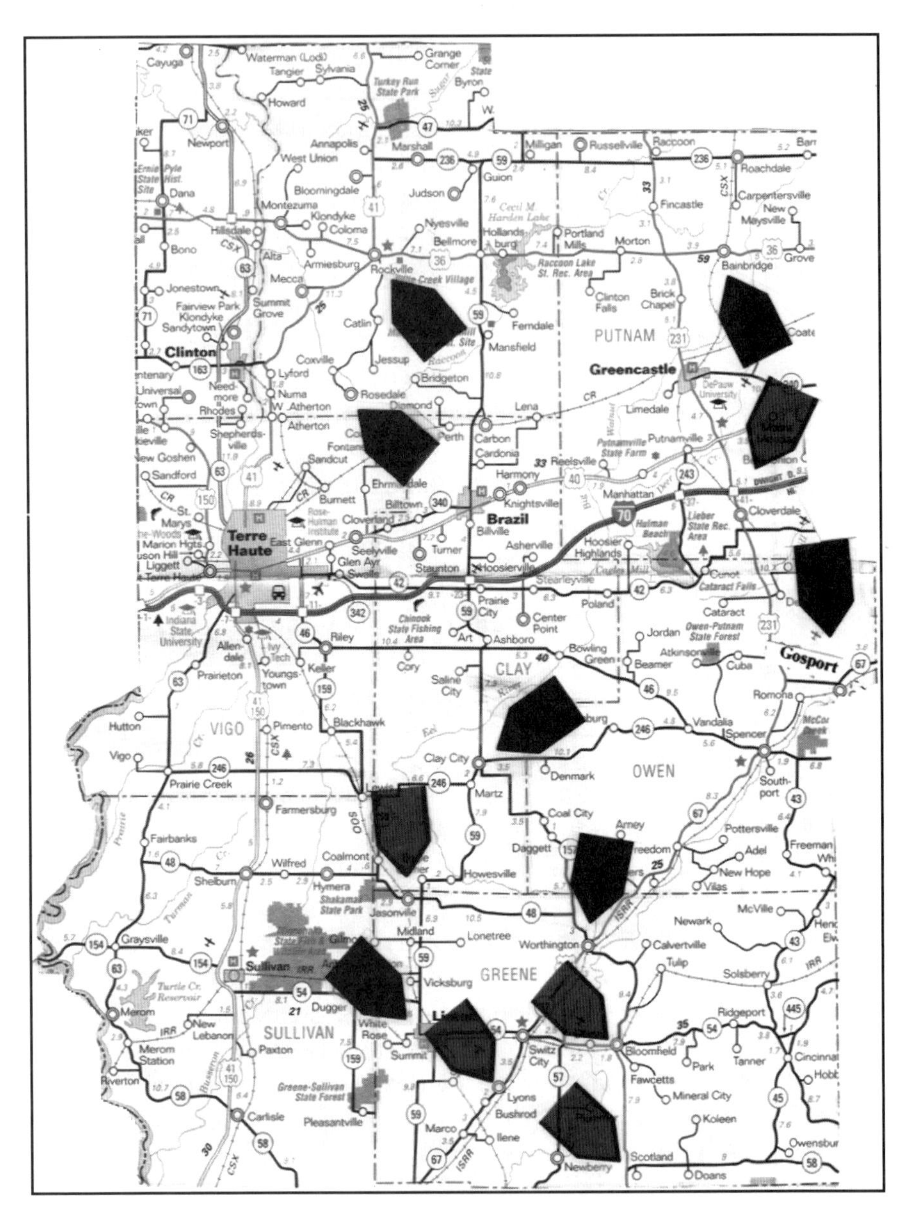


# DINERS — SOUTHWEST BY WEST

# SOUTHWEST BY WEST

## BAINBRIDGE

### THE BON-TON RESTAURANT

**110 West U. S. 36**

**(Town's main traffic artery)**

Some signs call it the Bon-Ton, others BonTon. Hyphen or no hyphen, the restaurant is more than a name. It has been a fixture in Bainbridge for years, the menu indicating since 1936.

Bon-Ton or BonTon, it is not the usual small town dinner. It's a block or two from the Bainbridge business area and it is not in a century old building. It is instead in a concrete block structure painted white with parking at the side.

We are too late for the morning coffee crowd, but the ham and cheese omelet, $3.85, is still available until 11 a.m. So are the two-eggs, sausage or bacon, hash browns or home fries, and biscuit or toast for $3.75.

The lunch bunch already is beginning to gather, the men in work clothes having started work early. They're hungry, ready to try the special of beef and noodles, mashed potatoes, cole slaw and coffee or tea for $4.76.

One man notes the size of his servings. "She must have thought I was hungry," he says of the cook, his voice showing no trace of disappointment.

There are no counters or booths. A twelve seat table is in the center of the dining room, eight seats at a round table and four seats at other tables. It is at the big table where men gather at dawn to begin their days.

This is a place to dine, not to eye the fixtures and decorations or rave about the decor. Those who prefer formal and stylish dining may not like the Bon-Ton, but workers, retirees and hungry motorists are apt to appreciate it.

# CLOVERDALE

## KAREN'S CAFE

### 3 East Market
### (One building off Main Street)

Forget the McDonald's and Hardee's up U.S. 231 at the I-70 interchange. Folks around Cloverdale like Karen's Cafe just fine.

The cafe occupies the lower level of a two-story building with a limestone veneer front from which three large windows open onto the street.

A sign on the door warns, "No shirt, no shoes, no service." The wall of the entrance appears to be a town bulletin board. It is covered with business cards, announcements and various information of interest to residents.

Inside, the dining room is spacious, with at least 60 seats at 14 tables, plus a few stools at a small counter beyond the tables. Walls are decorated with assorted crafts, which add to the decor. Pictures of rural scenes are along one wall. The ceiling is high as it is in most old buildings. The floor is covered with carpeting worn by the feet of loyal customers.

Except for two women at the counter, most of the customers at 7 a.m. are men. A bank employee shares one table with a retiree and a maintenance supervisor. Workers at various jobs are at other tables. There is friendly banter and endless barbs, which are returned with cordial retorts.

There is laughter amid the convivial atmosphere, but it remains in good taste. A sign near the cash register sees to that. It reads, "No loud abusive language or behavior will be tolerated. We reserve the right to refuse service."

The biscuits and gravy are good, so is the oatmeal, home cooked from scratch, not poured from a box, heated in a microwave and stirred. A pleasant waitress makes sure coffee cups are refilled before being emptied.

Karen's (for owner Karen Haltom) is open from 6 a.m. to 5 p.m. Mondays through Fridays and from 6 a.m. to 6:30 p.m. on Saturdays. It is closed Sundays. And it's just five minutes from the Interstate.

# ROCKVILLE

## WEBER'S FAMILY RESTAURANT

### 105 South Jefferson Street

Put the emphasis on "Family" in this pleasant and spacious restaurant on Courthouse Square in Rockville.

Take a seat inside and you get a glimpse of why. A message from management to customers reads:

"The Weber Family has been residents of Parke County for over 14 years. We have over 50 years of combined experience in the food and beverage business. We feel it is time that our community should have a restaurant that serves quality home cooked foods in a pleasant atmosphere, all at moderate prices.

"Your comments as to how we can improve our operation is very important. Our family has been taking care of customers for many years and we know our customers come first."

The Webers are Dick and Juanita. Manager Tina Brattain says, "Our restaurant is family owned and operated. Either me or my mother are here every day cooking." And every day means every day of the week.

The restaurant is open from 6 a.m. to 9 p.m. Mondays through Saturdays and from 7 a.m. to 4 p.m. Sundays.

Weber's is in a two-story building on the east side of the Parke County Courthouse. Wood panels on the front make an attractive appearance, which is an indication of the nice decor inside. Paintings of area scenes by local artists are on the walls.

This is not the usual small town diner. It is larger, much larger, with seats for 160 diners in two dining areas.

It's a little more formal than most small town cafes, but casual enough for two men to keep their hats on while eating breakfast. The clientele is diverse for the restaurant's customers include farmers, business men and women, professionals and a lot of customers who come to town for events such as the Covered Bridge Festival and the maple syrup season.

Omelets are among the morning selections, one with three eggs is $3.25, those with bacon, sausage or ham are $4.25. All other breakfast items are available.

The lunch special on this day is chicken pot pie with one side for $5.25. Country fried steak with three sides is the same price. Two daily lunch specials are available.

Specialties cited by Tina Brattain include evening buffets on Wednesday and Fridays as well as for Sunday lunches. "All you can eat" specials are available on Tuesdays and Thursdays.

For breakfast, lunch or dinner, or for banquets with up to 100 guests, this is a Parke County favorite.

## CLAY CITY

### MAIN STREET PIZZA AND FAMILY DINING

**Main Street**

Don't let the "pizza" in this diner's name detract you from stopping. This is a full-service restaurant in the heart of Clay City's small commercial district.

From the outside, there is little impressive about the place, a one-story brick between two other business buildings. And the interior is nothing special. The floor is covered in inlaid tile, the concrete walls painted light yellow above the paneling at the bottom.

The dining area is about 30 feet wide and deep, the kitchen at the rear. Tables, with seats for 40 to 50 diners, are covered with Formica.

So much for the looks of the place. It is the food that attracts residents. Many of the seats are taken at 8:15 a.m. Chances are it was even busier after the 6 a.m. opening when farmers and other workers stopped by en route to work.

Most of the customers appear to be a part of the regular crowd which makes it a habit to stop by each morning, swap stories and catch up on what has been happening around town.

A late arrival is greeted by three women at one table who invite him to "sit down and pick up the check." He ignores the remark, joins them, and the conversation resumes, accented by a man's point of view.

He and other customers can chose from a variety of breakfast items on the menu. The "Ultimate Breakfast," for example, includes two eggs with bacon, sausage or ham, hash browns, a pancake or French toast. The $4.95 meal is enough to keep a farmer contented until lunch when he can choose the buffet or order sandwiches like a cheeseburger for $1.89 or chicken fillet for the same price.

Formality at this Clay County cafe on Ind. 59 is just a word in a dictionary. It doesn't apply here or in many other small town diners. This is down home country, a place where a woman customer enters with a home-canned jar of jam for her restaurant served toast.

If you see a man walk out of the restroom smiling, he probably is from out of town and has seen the sign over the stool for the first time. It reads, "If you sprinkle/when you tinkle/be a sweetie/and wipe the seatie (or anything else)."

One thing this place doesn't have is pretense.

## JASONVILLE

### SHARON'S KOUNTRY KITCHEN

**East Main**

It's hard to overlook Sharon's Kountry Kitchen. A large banner on the north side of Ind. 48 at the east side of town calls attention to the downtown diner several blocks ahead. Which is good! This is not a place to miss.

It is worth a stop, good food aside. The decor alone is worth a trip to this old-mining town.

Like many Main Street diners, this one, too, is in a corner two-story brick, but there is little reminder of the building's age once inside. The floor is carpeted, the furniture sturdy. The tables are covered, the paneled walls are decorated with plaques, posters and dozens of pictures of the Jasonville of an earlier time when coal was the city's main industry.

Longaberger baskets are on display as are snap on tool collectibles.

Owners Sharon and William Boyd bought the restaurant from Sharon's brother, Dick Klein in 1997. A framed news story explains what Sharon had in mind when she took over the business. "I thought it would be exciting and fun. And I have not been disappointed. I've renewed old friendships and started new ones."

The colorful menus offer extensive selections for all meals. The "Farmer's Breakfast," served all day, includes two eggs, any style, hash browns, bacon, ham or sausage, toast or biscuits and coffee for $4.75.

Sharon Boyd lists among the Kountry Kitchen specialties her barbecued baby back ribs, steaks and breakfasts. "We have a full, big menu and all our food is home cooked... no mixes or pre-fixed items.

"We had not been in the restaurant business until we bought this place, but with my love to cook, my desire to meet the public and my husband's bookkeeping and office work, it has worked out well."

The Kountry Kitchen is open from 5:30 a.m. to 9 p.m. Mondays through Saturdays and from 6 a.m. to 2 p.m. on Sundays.

Among its customers are farmers, coal miners, families, business people, professional women and visitors who come through town to visit nearby Shakamak State Park. Most of them probably enjoy the food and service as much as Sharon Boyd likes operating the business.

She notes, "If you start with honesty, cleanliness and good service, and quality food, I don't see where you can go wrong. Love, labor and laughter. That sums it up."

A sign near the cash register is part of that levity. It reads, "If Mama B ain't happy, ain't nobody happy."

So far, "Mama B" appears to be extremely happy.

## SHAKAMAK FAMILY RESTAURNANT

### West Main

This restaurant, also known as Hometown Heritage, is just a block from Sharon's. It, too, is on the ground floor of a two-story brick. We were unable to stop at this diner and the operator did not return our request for information.

# BLOOMFIELD

## CARDINAL CAFE

### 24 East Main Street

Diners at the Cardinal Cafe can enjoy the food, appreciate the atmosphere and keep at eye on Greene County government, all at the same time.

On the north side of Courthouse Square, the cafe is bright and cheerful with a spaciousness seldom seen in small town cafes in old buildings. And the building, indeed, is old. The high ceiling in the street-level restaurant is covered with hammered metal, perhaps copper, a kind that was popular a hundred years ago.

Huge windows face the street. Crafts are on display in cases near the entrance. The huge dining area has tables for 60, maybe 70, diners without being cramped. There are no booths, no stools and no counter. The walls are painted above patterned wallpaper which extends up four feet from the floor.

Pictures on the wall, painted by local artists, are for sale. A poster of Bob Knight, the Indiana University basketball coach, is on the wall as are pennants for West Point and Kentucky. There is no indication of support for Purdue University teams which are arch rivals of those from I.U.

The cafe's name, too, has a link to sports, the athletic teams from Bloomfield High being the Cardinals.

It is mid-morning but some customers are in the restaurant ordering breakfast which is served until 11 a.m. Western omelets at $4.35 are a breakfast special. We order biscuits and gravy, which is $1.75, and oatmeal, which is $1.45, but these are just a few of the options available. Coffee is 60 cents, a bargain compared to those at some diners.

"You have to keep your prices lower in small towns. Everyone thinks food prices at restaurants should be cheap, but I have to pay the same for it as the guys in downtown Indianapolis do," explains J. R. Davis, who owns the cafe with his wife, Sherri.

The cafe is open from 6 a.m. to 2 p.m. Mondays through Fridays and from 6 a.m. to 10:30 a.m. on Saturdays.

On the lunch menu this day are meatloaf with mashed potatoes and gravy, macaroni and cheese and a roll for $4.25. A meatloaf Manhattan is $3.95. The roast beef Manhattan and turkey club are each $3.95.

Davis got his first taste of the restaurant business back in high school when he was a cook as part of a work-study program at Crane (a nearby naval weapons center). He and a cousin, Dallas Parsley, owned the Shawnee Trail restaurant, which their mothers had run earlier, from 1993 to 1996.

"The restaurant business gets in your blood," he explains, which is why he and Sherri have owned the Cardinal Cafe since February, 1997. "It has done really well," he adds.

Among the reasons for its success is Stacey, a red-haired waitress. "Everyone loves Stacey. It is amazing. Customers bring her presents at Christmas and now that she is expecting a baby, they bring things for the child. She is one of those people customers love to death," the Davises agree.

The downtown cafe is different from the Shawnee Trail, which is a few miles from Bloomfield. "Some of my old customers won't come into the Cardinal because it is in town. They think it is a little more fancy, which it is not. A lot of our customers at the Shawnee Trail were farmers. Here at the Cardinal Cafe we get more of the Courthouse crowd and people who work around the Square," Davis explains.

Breakfast, he adds, is a big meal at the cafe. "We usually have people knocking on the door before we open at 6 a.m. It means a lot to have people show up every single day. They can gather, talk and have a good time. We get to know a lot of people, which is what I like best about the business."

A poignant letter that appeared in the *Bloomfield Evening World* tells a lot about the restaurant and its customers. Writer Oneta Noel relates a visit to the restaurant with her husband and her sister:

"Our waitress was friendly, caring and hospitable in every way. When she was filling my husband Marion's coffee cup, my sister, ever the teacher, told her, 'Let me make a suggestion. He cannot see that you just added coffee to his cup. You should alert a blind person so he will not burn himself.' This waitress accepted the advice graciously and was exceptional in all her service."

The letter explains that Kent Benson, an all-American who helped lead Indiana University to the 1976 national basketball championship, was a guest in the restaurant at the time. It continues:

"Kent removed his championship ring and moved my husband Marion's finger over it, explaining the date and every emblem on it. Just before we exited, Marion said, 'I'm a minister and I must ask if you are a born again Christian?'

"Kent wrapped those long arms around my darling of 51 years and said, 'Oh, yes, sir! I am, indeed, and God leads my life.' He then signed a picture to Marion with Romans, 8:28."

The letter concluded: "What an exciting morning! And it all began with an outstanding breakfast and waitress in our local Cardinal Cafe."

It ended, "May I recommend the western omelet."

That kind of advertising can't be bought.

## LINTON

### THE GRILL

**60 A Street Northeast (A is one of Linton's main streets)**

Back at Cloverdale on another day, a waitress has told us to be sure to stop at Jim Cary's diner in her home town of Linton. "It's called The Grill and you will like it," she had said.

It is 10:15 a.m. and we have followed her advice. The Grill is still more than half full, indicating that breakfast is a big attraction.

It is obvious this is a busy diner. And one that is neat and clean with an atmosphere where bankers, doctors, mine workers, businessmen, farmers, retirees and tourists can feel at ease in each other's company.

Linton is an old coal town, a heritage reflected in the "United Mine Workers of America" engraving on a clock on one of the walls. Not far away is another clock, its I.U. logo reflecting both labor and management's support for Indiana University athletic teams.

Smoking is allowed, which, as we have found, is common in most diners on Indiana's main streets, but the air seems pure. The Grill is neat and clean. Its walls are papered above three feet high paneling painted a tasteful green.

The menu is extensive, offering a wide breakfast selection which keeps patrons returning day after day. Coffee cups are never empty; the pleasant waitresses see to that.

Coffee is included with the price of most breakfast items which are served anytime. A full order of biscuits and gravy, with coffee, is $2.25. Three hotcakes with two eggs and coffee are $3.95. Two eggs with bacon, ham or sausage (and coffee) are $3.25. Omelets range in price from $3.25 for a cheese to $3.95 for the western, coffee included.

In addition to the breakfast items, the restaurant specialties are the sandwiches and rib-eye steaks cooked outside. The twelve-ounce rib-eye dinner with choice of potato and bread is $11.95. Basket specials including chicken strips with French fries and cole slaw are $5.50.

And everything, Jim Cary, explains is fresh and prepared to order.

The Grill is not just any small town diner. And owner Jim Cary is not just any owner. He was, a plaque on a wall notes, “an honored professional among executives and businessmen” in the 1997-98 edition of the *American directory of Who’s Who.*

A restaurant has been at the location since 1922, Cary the owner since 1986. The Grill is open from 5 a.m. to 7 p.m. Mondays through Thursdays; from 5 a.m. to 8 p.m. Fridays and Saturdays, and from 5 a.m. to 2 p.m. Sundays. It is closed only for Thanksgiving and Christmas.

Cary has had a lot of experiences over the last 14 years, but none likely is more memorable—or more humorous—than one that involved a 17-year-old honor student hired as a waitress. Soon after coming to work she asked, “How do you make toast?”

“She wasn’t here long,” Cary adds.

If you stop at The Grill now, you will find knowledgeable servers and a pleasant atmosphere.

# GOSPORT

## GOSPORT DINER

### 23 North Main Street

Every town should be so fortunate. The Gosport Diner in the center of town is a restaurant that makes stops in small towns a delight for hungry motorists.

It is especially so for railroad buffs. "The Gosport Diner" sign out front is accented with a railroad crossing symbol. The railroad motif continues inside the door. Among a score of old pictures are many railroad scenes. A mural of the old Gosport train station, complete with water tank, covers part of the back wall with a "Monon" notation.

(The Monon Railroad was called the Hoosier Line as it rumbled across the state from the Ohio River toward Chicago. It was the lifeline of commerce for towns such as Gosport.)

A reproduction of a page from an old newspaper is among the exhibits in the tastefully decorated diner. Walls are plastered to the high ceiling, from where six flower containers hang. A row of fluorescent lights illuminate the dining room.

The diner, owned by Floyd and Donna Friend, appears spotless, enough so to have earned it recognition as Owen County's cleanest restaurant.

The menus are tastefully decorated with, of course, graphics of railroad scenes, locomotives, tracks and the Monon Station. But the menus are more than attractive. They are extensive and the prices reasonable.

The breakfast special of two eggs, toast, sausage or bacon and a half order of biscuits and gravy is $3.65. A half order of biscuits and gravy is enough for us. It is as big as many full orders and much better than most.

It is not surprising that some of the locals come back morning after morning for breakfast. At 8 a.m. six men are at one table, couples at two more and a few other men at booths.

The men at the front table are talking, of course, about Indiana basketball. They are in their 60s and they boast of youthful greatness that probably has grown in their imagination over the last 40 years. Oh, they talk about other issues of the day, too, issues like the caucus to select candidates for the Gosport Town Council the previous night.

One of the men is Ned Smith, a long-time acquaintance and a retired school superintendent. He explains the history and significance of the murals and pictures.

If the men return for lunch they can order the $3.95 special, which is chicken and noodles with two sides that can be chosen from among green beans, slaw, cucumbers and onions or pickled beets. Other specialties of the diner are ham and beans and fish.

Donna Friend says cheap prices and the homemade specials make the Gosport Diner different from other restaurants in the area. Plus, she adds, "All our customers. They are unique."

And she should have boasted about her pies and cheese cake, having related this experience: "It wasn't funny at the time, but burglars broke in one night and stole the cash register and a pie and cheese cake. When caught they admitted they had enjoyed the pie and cheesecake. The joke around town after that was that thieves were breaking into the Gosport Diner for Donna's desserts."

The judge gave the two men three-year terms, one year for each penny that was in the cash register.

Mrs. Friend says Gosport reminds her of author Stephen King's novel *Castle Rock*. It should be pointed out, however, that there is nothing scary about the Gosport Diner.

## WORTHINGTON

### THE FRONT PORCH

**118 Canal Street**
**(Ind. 67 through town)**

This is a restaurant aptly named for it is a front porch onto the passing traffic on Ind. 67, Worthington's main traffic artery.

And the restaurant indeed has a front porch. Two swings glide from chains that fasten to the ceiling of the roof that stretches across the front of the block building painted brown.

And for those who prefer to sit rather than swing, a long bench also is on the porch, indicating guests can relax after a meal or sit comfortably in case there is a wait for a table.

The Front Porch has become a popular diner in a few short years, attracting area residents as well as motorists on Ind. 67 that connects Indianapolis to the northeast, Vincennes to the southwest.

A sign out front identifies the place as the "Front Porch Steakhouse - Country Cookin'." Another notation on the door cautions that neither checks nor credit cards are accepted so visitors should plan to have cash when they stop.

Inside, the walls of block are painted blue and off white. Plastered cathedral ceilings add to the spaciousness of the three dining areas. Jugs of the pottery kind, crocks and glass jars are on a shelf over the front door.

It's a friendly place at this mid-morning hour. Only a few late breakfast customers remain and there is time for the servers to relax.

"Speak of the devil," one waitress says as a regular customer walks in. She orders him to sit down. He asks for coffee. The server allows as how she will "mosey on out" to get it.

This is a full service restaurant with a menu to cover breakfast, lunch or dinner. Consider this breakfast item for the famished: "Ten ounce New York strip steak, two eggs, hash browns and toast—$6.95." Or this for the working man: "Five ounce sirloin and two eggs, hash browns and toast—$4.95." And for a retiree with no physical labor ahead: "Two eggs, toast and hash browns or grits, $2.79."

If the regular menu daily doesn't suffice, diners can return on Friday and Saturday nights for the prime rib or seafood.

This is a down home, front porch place without pretense where good food is served in comfortable surroundings by pleasant waitresses.

# LYONS

## THE TOWNE HOUSE RESTAURANT

### Ind. 67 South (In Lyons business area)

By the time this is read, the Towne House may be in a new home at the edge of Lyons. If so, customers can expect the same standards maintained by owners Kevin and Melinda Brown for more than 20 years.

"We have always prepared and served our food with care and quality and will continue to improve and provide quality food in the new facility," Kevin Brown promises.

The restaurant remained in its old location throughout 1999, a one-story brick with cedar shakes on a roof that extended about four feet over the sidewalk. A bulletin board of sorts is at the entrance for the promotion of events in the Greene County town.

Hours may change with the move, but it was open at its mid-town location from 7 a.m. to 2 p.m. Mondays, 7 a.m. to 9 p.m. Tuesdays through Saturdays and from 11 a.m. to 9 p.m. Sundays.

This is a restaurant, regardless of the location, that boasts: "Home cooking at its finest. Let us do the baking—homemade pies and bread." It's a service not many restaurants can provide.

The attractive covered menu offers a full breakfast selection, along with that bread which is baked on the spot. It is 9:40 and the local breakfast crowd has left, ready to face the day. Among those who remain is a couple traveling new routes through southern Indiana. They order, then open a map to sketch their drive around the state.

At an earlier hour, the diners would have included farmers, professional men and women, businessmen and retirees.

Huge pictures of two L & M High School basketball teams, including the one that reached the semistate finals in 1985 before a loss to Southridge. L & M, itself a consolidation of Lyons and Marco, later was absorbed into a consolidation called White River Valley.

Kevin Brown notes the new restaurant will be a "new facility with a new look and a new menu." Basketball fans likely hope it includes pictures of those two L & M teams.

# SCOTLAND

## TOODIE'S, TOO CAFE

### Main Street

We were so impressed with Toodie's, Too we returned a few weeks later. We were disappointed when we saw it was no longer open and only this sign marked its discontinuance:

"Due to circumstances beyond my control, wc are closed. I am truly sorry and have appreciated your friendship first, and your patronage at Toodie's, Too."

It was signed "Cathy."

For those who have visited Toodie's, Too, those who might have or those who may if the restaurant ever reopens, these are our observations from the earlier visit.

* * *

You won't find a number on this Main Street establishment in Scotland. The town, a mile to the east of Ind. 58, is too small to worry about such formalities. Besides, most folks know where it is, anyhow.

We first visited Toodie's back in 1993 when it was owned by Harold and Edna Manis, who maintained the business for almost 25 years before it was closed in the mid-1990s.

Except for the post office, it appears to be the only meeting place in Scotland.

Cathy Lester reopened the restaurant in 1997, giving a new look to the diner in its old white concrete block building. On this October morning in 1999, four pickups and two cars are parked out front. It is again an oasis for farmers and other workers as it was back when the Manises owned it.

The old Mail Pouch thermometer remains at the entrance. Flowers are in two old milk cans. A flower bed is to the left of the double door entrance. The inside is neat and clean.

The friendliness remains. "Good morning, Bobbi," a man says as he enters. "Morning, Joe, Joe," he is greeted in return.

It is 6:30 and three diners are at the six stools at the counter. A few other men are at the three four-seat tables. Another dining area is off to the side, but it is not in use at this early hour.

We choose a half order of biscuits and gravy. It's as big as most full orders and good enough to lure us back as it does the regular customers.

Joe, by now, has joined the conversation with his friends. "Need some more coffee, Joe?" he is asked. The waitress is also the cook but she has time to be friendly and no order is delayed.

This is rural Indiana and the decor is to match. Two old seed corn sacks hang on a wall. Shelves hold model farm equipment; one for John Deere tractors, another for Farmalls. An International pedal wheel tractor is on display as is a display case full of old model cars, trucks, wagons and other conveyances.

A spirit or community is obvious. The annual Scotland Festival is the third Saturday in September and a container for contributions to finance it is near the entrance. And a sign notes the restaurant will not open until 9 a.m. the first Saturday of each month. "Please patronize the Breakfast Club at the Fire Station," customers are told.

The men drift off one by one. There is work to be done. But they will be back tomorrow and other mornings to come.

* * *

It will be Scotland's gain if Toodie's, Too ever reopens.

## SHOALS

### VELMA'S DINER

**Main Street**

A restaurant has been on Main Street south of U.S. 50 in Shoals for so long it doesn't need a street number. Just ask anyone in sight and he or she will point the way.

Velma's has been the name on the restaurant in downtown Shoals for the last sixteen years. And the location on the east side of Main Street had been a diner for almost sixty years before that.

Velma is Velma L. Sharp, who says it is the home cooked meals and pies that bring customers back day after day, seven days a week. An average of 200 diners stop daily, some for breakfast, some for dinner, the majority for lunch.

This is small town Indiana and Shoals, like the diner, remains much now like it has been for decades. Except for the Bo-Mac's, an old-type drive-in, there are no other restaurants in Shoals. The closest fast food outlet is a new McDonald's at Loogootee nine miles away. That's why, no matter the time, be it the opening at 5 a.m. or the closing at 7 p.m. you will likely find diners at Velma's.

McDonald's are impersonal. Velma's is a sit back, relax, talk with a neighbor or friend operation.

It is not a state-of-the-art cafe. It remains much as it has for years, with seats for 50 customers at 12 tables. Chances are most of the customers have been coming here for so long they wouldn't be comfortable amid the glitz and glamour of a trendy restaurant where meals are prepared in advance, zapped in a microwave and served by waitresses in identical uniforms.

But it is a place for local residents to stop, find a seat, relax, be waited on, then served by someone they've likely known for years. And they can learn in the meantime about everything that's going on around town, be it the debate over whether a prison should be at the edge of town or comments about the Shoals High School Jug Rox basketball team.

If you are driving through Shoals, attending the annual July Catfish Festival or looking for the famed Jug Rox up on the hill, take time to stop at Velma's. It's a reminder of what all small towns once had...and a look at what Shoals still has.

# ODON

## THE ESSEN HAUS

### 101 East Main

Business cards for Bob and Leann Wagler's Essen Haus undersell its attractions. "Buffet, salads, desserts," the cards note.

The Essen Haus, in a two-story building at Odon's main intersection, is much more than that. Consider these observations noted at an 8 a.m. stop on a September weekday:

Eight men, including a state trooper in uniform, are at one table, four other men are at a smaller table next to them. Other

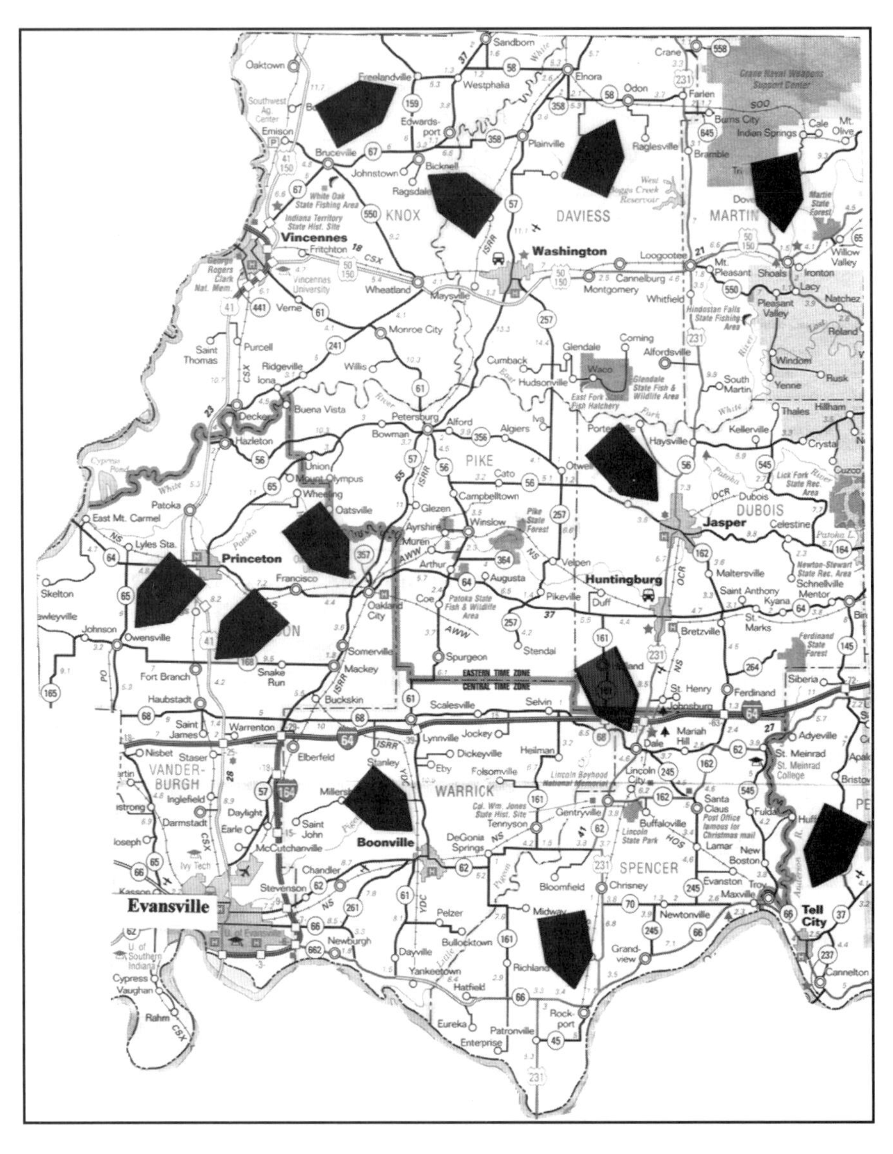


tables are occupied, so are some of the booths. Some of the diners are husbands and wives, this being a place for families.

There are still vacant seats for the dining room is spacious—big enough to seat at least 80 customers. But for a small town (Odon's population is 1,500), the restaurant is busier than could be expected at this time of day.

It is a place where diners go from table to table as they enter, address each by their first names. Strangers are greeted with nods and smiles.

A senior citizen, obviously a regular visitor, enters and is greeted with, "Well, you made it through another night." He jokes that he is ready for another day, noting his obituary is not in the morning newspapers.

The decor is pleasing. The tables and booths are covered. A strip of wallpaper divides the darker and lighter paneling on the walls. On display atop a shelf across the kitchen area are old crocks, canning jars, crafts and flowers. A quilt hangs under a shelf on a side wall.

Waitress are dressed in maroon aprons over white uniforms, their hair covered. They are pleasant, greet diners almost as soon as they are seated and fill coffee cups without being asked.

The Waglers have made Amish cooking a specialty of the restaurant, which each day attracts 300 to 350 diners, "farmers, factory workers, businessmen and women, doctors and lawyers . . . all types of people," the Waglers say.

We order oatmeal. It is excellent, made on the spot, not poured from a bag and heated in the microwave. Other breakfast options include steak, two eggs and toast for $3.75. Ham, two eggs and toast are $2.99. The "Sunrise Skillet," eggs, sausage, potatoes, cheese and gravy, is $3.25 as is the western omelet.

This is a wide-variety menu that includes cinnamon rolls, bagels, grits and breakfast sandwiches.

For those who return for lunch, the buffet is $4.95. The Friday evening dinner special, with hot bar, salad bar, dessert and drink, is $6.95.

The Essen Haus is open from 5:30 a.m. to 2 p.m. Mondays through Thursdays. The hours are 5:30 a.m. to 8 p.m. on Fridays and 5:30 a.m. to 2 p.m. on Saturdays.

To find the Essen Haus drive south from Ind. 58 to the center of town and look for the awning across the front at the main corner of the business district. You won't find many better places to stop for breakfast or lunch in southwestern Indiana.

# FREELANDVILLE

## THE DUTCHMAN

### Corner of Ind. 58 and Ind. 159
### (Town's main intersection)

Credit some farmers from around town for the restaurant in Freelandville.

To make sure they'd have a place to gather over coffee each morning, they formed a corporation known as the Krop Krew, bought the building and offered it rent free to an operator.

The Dutchman is on the street level floor of a two-story brick, whose windows on the upper floor are boarded. It's obvious the owners of the building care about a restaurant. Chances are they aren't interested in restoring the upper floor for apartments or for businesses.

The restaurant operation has been owned by Dewey Hartsburg and Bruce Pepmeier since the mid 1990s. Virginia Held is the manager and, on this day, our server.

Formality is just a word in a dictionary here. She wears a T-shirt and shorts and never lets a visitor leave as a stranger. She greets us with a pleasant "Good morning." Another customer enters. "Walt," she calls him, knowing most of the folks who enter.

"Walt" sits near six men at a big table and is served coffee before he asks for a cup. "Anyone want more coffee?" the others are asked.

Some of the men likely are members of the "Krop Krew." They obviously are farmers or were before they retired. One wears a hat that promotes "the other white meat," indicating he's a pork producer. Other men wear caps promoting farm supply distributors. It is a harmonious group.

There is little luxurious about The Dutchman. A side door opens onto the Ind. 58 side of the restaurant, the main door ajar, a screen door in place. The ceilings are high, the floor covered in tile, the walls paneled.

The restaurant is for service, not for pretense. "We are nothing fancy," says Mrs. Held. "We just try to serve good food and please our customers."

Prices are reasonable. The breakfast special is a bacon and cheese omelet with toast, $2.19. Other selections are available. And, of course, there is the coffee and the conversation, which are among the returns the Krop Krew receives on its investment.

"Business," Mrs. Held says, "is good enough to keep the doors open."

Chances are it's a bit better than that. She notes the turnout is good on Wednesday nights when catfish is on the menu and again on Friday nights when fried chicken is the special. "Those nights, folks drive over from Daviess County and other nearby areas to savor the food," she adds, pleasantly, of course.

# BICKNELL

## DODIE'S PANTRY

### 204 North Main Street

If at first you don't find Dodie's Pantry, look for the Union Planter's Bank. Dodie's is across Main Street, its only identification small lettering on the two windows facing the street.

For Bicknell area residents, Dodie's has been a landmark for years, back when it was down the street. It has been owned for the last 20 years by John R. Myers and Laura Lett, who is Dodie's daughter.

Despite the age of the two-story building, the diner is clean and neat. A border runs under the acoustical tile ceiling at the top of walls painted a light yellow. Table tops are bare except for two near the front which are covered. A line of fluorescent lights extend down the center.

It is quiet when we visit Dodie's at 8 a.m. Most of the early coffee gang is gone. A few men remain at the big table up front. Three men and a woman are near the front window. A man walks in alone. He is greeted with "Hi, Harold." He obviously is a regular customer.

We are told the crowd would have been larger and more vocal had we arrived earlier. "That's when everyone talks to everyone else at the same time. It doesn't matter if they are in the back or up front. They still yell across the room to each other," we are told.

Laura Lett describes her customers as “a lot of farmers, plus every other type person.” Including, she adds, the mayor and “Cindi, our clerk treasurer, who is a riot.” Cindi is Cindi Parkhill, who has been involved in many of the pantry’s humorous moments.

Dodie’s is open from 4 a.m. to 7 p.m. Mondays through Fridays and from 4 a.m. to 6 p.m. Saturdays. That is 99 hours a week, which explains why the restaurant is closed on Sundays.

The breakfast menu is typical of most small town diners. For lunch, the country fried steak (a specialty of Dodie’s), mashed or fried potatoes, homemade cole slaw and a roll is just $2.99. “Almost everything,” Laura Lett adds, “is homemade, including the pies.”

This is a diner where the servers may also be dishwashers. A sign in kitchen advises employees, “Dishes are for everyone. When customers are taken care of there are always dishes.”

## JASPER

### ANN’S PLACE
**617 Main Street**

Ann Eckert has a window onto the world that is downtown Jasper from her diner at the northwest corner of the Dubois County Courthouse Circle.

She has a view to Main Street and to the circular drive that forms the center of town.

“We see too much at times,” she laughs, but admits, “Every day is interesting at A.P.’s (Ann’s Place). You never know what may happen when you open the door. The atmosphere is different every day.

“It is,” she adds, “a fun place to dine, hang out or what not. Be they alone or with a group, we welcome all customers as soon as they enter. I love my business and every one of my customers gets a special place in my heart."

And that's if they arrive for coffee before dawn or show up near closing.

Ann doesn't look old enough to be among Jasper's entrepreneurs, but she has owned the little restaurant for 12 years.

Open from 5 a.m. to 4:30 p.m. daily except Sundays, Ann's Place remains as popular as ever. It is just after the noon rush, but a number of customers remain, although, Ann says, business on this day has been slower than usual.

She serves customers while her mother works at the grill behind the counter. It is Mom who comes up with some of the homemade soups and sandwiches that have made Ann's Place a popular stop. Consider the rieble soup on the menu. "It's made with a dropped dumpling," Ann explains.

The diner is small, actually tiny, with but 36 seats, including stools at a counter. The windows on two sides and a high ceiling, however, make the place look larger.

This is a restaurant that's easy to find. Just locate the center of town and look for the yellow two-story Gutzweiler Building. Ann's Place is at the corner.

Diners who like a touch of atmosphere and a reminder of small town diners of the mid-1900s will enjoy a stop at Ann's Place.

## OAKLAND CITY

### Genny's Country Kitchen
### 239 North Main Street

Okay! Okay! We know this is a book about restaurants where Hoosiers start their days. Genny's Country Kitchen doesn't open until 10:30 a.m. but we are including it anyhow.

Some folks may wait to start their days at that hour, anyhow.

It is closed on Mondays, a day we stopped at the little diner in a two-story yellow brick that is trimmed in blue. It was our loss for the restaurant features home cooking and daily buffets.

Owned by Lavon Helsley, it is open only from the 10:30 start until its 2 p.m. close.

The mid-town location appears convenient. It's close enough for residents in town to come on foot and near enough to Ind. 57 and Ind. 65 for motorists to make a quick detour.

Not having dined at the Country Kitchen, we've chosen to excerpt a letter written to the *Princeton Daily Clarion* by someone who did stop for lunch. Here in part is what William F. Connor of Princeton wrote:

"Parking our car along a little stone sidewalk, we entered the past. The hardwood floor was clean and shined by use and age. The fragrance of fresh baked apple pie floated in the air.

"From the tall ceiling came the hum of a half dozen ceiling fans. From long chains hung milk white globes emitting a soft light reminiscent of moonlight.

"After my second trip through the line I still had not sampled all of the different varieties of food. I did, however, manage to have pieces of raisin pie and apple pie and a small helping of cobbler.

"My wife assured me that a bowl of beans she had was the best beans she had tasted since she had last sampled her mother's cooking."

Connor mentioned the bill for he and his wife was $10. But he added, "The return to my youth was far more valuable than $10. The food was wonderful, but the experience is beyond price."

It was a praise any restaurant owner would appreciate.

## FORT BRANCH

### CODY'S CAFE

**112 Railroad Street**

Most restaurants serve food. This one serves food and character. And there is always a chance you also may meet some of the town characters when you stop by.

The location is, indeed, on Railroad Street, a narrow drive between the north-south railroad tracks and the restaurant. A long train delays us at the tracks which divide the cafe from a parking area and a newer section of Fort Branch's business district. Diners can park in the lot, then cross the tracks to the diner in the center of what looks to be the Gibson County town's oldest block.

One of the Fort Branch's older residents says the cafe has been here "a long, long time." It looks it, its age adding to its flavor. Its hours are long, 4 a.m. to 8 p.m. Mondays through Fridays; 4 a.m. to 1 p.m. Saturdays and Sundays.

This is not one of those fancy diners. Anyone who prefers gentility and style need not enter. It doesn't look impressive from the outside, its exterior covered in aluminum siding. Nor is it elaborate inside.

Superficiality is for fast food restaurants at the edges of other towns. It doesn't apply to Cody Selby's restaurant, which is no more than 15 feet wide with just enough stools and tables to seat 24 diners.

Except for some pictures and flower pots that hang from the low ceiling there are few decorations. Paneling extends three feet up the walls, which are then painted light green.

A sign in the work area behind the counter says, "Fresh watermelon. No seed spitting." If it isn't a joke, no one is eating melons or spitting seeds, anyhow. Another sign. "Coffee 10c," also is a joke, outdated by inflation not of the cafe's making.

A smaller sign notes, "Today's menu—No. 1 take it. No. 2 leave it." You soon get the idea the place doesn't take itself too seriously.

That doesn't stop customers from returning, again and again. We enter the cafe at 4 p.m. Seven men and one woman occupy eight of the nine stools at the counter, most of whom talk softly as they sip coffee and soft drinks.

It is a quiet place until someone feeds the jukebox, making conversation difficult. The sound mutes the conversation Rosie O'Donnell is in with her guests on the TV back in the corner.

We choose a table where a pleasant waitress brings us a telephone book we have asked to see. She is as courteous to her regular guests as she is to strangers.

"It is a busy place," she says, "especially in the mornings. This is where people come to socialize and settle the world's problems. Saturday mornings are especially big. There were so many people in here last Saturday, it was difficult to find a seat."

They came then—and on other days—for such menu items as bacon and eggs, $2.75, full orders of biscuits and gravy, $2, and ham and cheese omelets, $4.

They can return later for the hamburger steak, mashed potatoes, corn and a drink for $4.60. Or for sandwiches such as barbecue for $1.75.

And, then, there is also the specialty, "the famed Cody Burger." After all, this is its home.

## OWENSVILLE

### OWENSVILLE CAFE

**115 South Main Street**

Owner Nancy Moore laughs when asked what makes the Owensville Cafe different from other diners in the Owensville area. Then she adds:

"It's the only one in town." More about that later.

It also may be the only restaurant around that has a philosophy. A sign on display offers this bit to wisdom: "When you quit getting better, you'll soon stop being good."

Nancy and Bill Moore bought the cafe, which a waitress says has been "around forever," in 1993. It's in a brick building with a stone facing that rises three feet from the sidewalk. The wood trim is painted red. Short lace curtains are atop the front windows that have Venetian blinds.

The cafe is open from 6 a.m. to 2 p.m. Mondays through Saturdays and from 4 a.m. to 2 p.m. on Sundays. The customers are mostly farmers and local residents and everyone seems to know everyone else. "It's a place most people like to come to at least once a day. Some are here more often than that," says Mrs. Moore.

We stop at the restaurant at 8 a.m. on a weekday morning. Two men are at a community table. One is working the crossword puzzle in the morning paper. A waitress asks the other what he has planned for the day.

"Not much," he says, knowing he is always welcome at the Owensville Cafe if he gets bored at home. By the time he has finished the sentence another senior citizen returns for his second visit of the morning.

The waitress notes that breakfast is served any time. "That's never a problem," she adds.

Mrs. Moore, though, isn't one to boast. The breakfast menu, she says, is "about the same as any other diner around... eggs, hash browns. We don't have specials with names." Eggs and bacon with hash browns and toast are $3.00. Omelets average about $3.25.

Lunch specials with two choices of meat are different each day. They include a vegetable, salad and dessert for $5.50.

About that "only restaurant in town" comment by Mrs. Moore: She doesn't want us to ignore any competition. A family pizza place is open in Owensville. It, too, is a place locals sometimes gather, the breakfast fare coffee and donuts.

But it's likely not a place that's open at 4 a.m. on Sundays where early risers can read the weekend newspaper, have coffee, then order a full breakfast if they choose.

## POSEYVILLE

### HAROLD'S RESTAURANT

**11 West Main Street**

If you like fine food and good service, you'll like Harold's Restaurant in Poseyville. If you also are a Coca Cola collector, you may never want to leave.

The restaurant in a yellow two-story brick building on Poseyville's Main Street (which also is Ind. 68) is filled with scores, make that hundreds, of Coca Cola items from the past to the present.

You may need to drive by a couple of times before you spot the small "Harold's Restaurant" that hangs out onto the street from the second level. Look, too, for the maroon awning that extends over the front of the restaurant which has a front of block glass, the kind seldom used today.

Inside, curtains decorate the top of the front windows. Two fans are gently circulating air from their anchors on the ceiling on this warm September morning.

Coke items are on the paneled walls, shelves and floor. An old Coca Cola cooler, the kind where pop bottles cooled in water and the tops were flipped off at the opener on the side, is on display.

So are a Coke sock cap, a Coke clock, a Coke apron and Coca Cola signs, pictures, bottles and glasses. If a Coca Cola item has been made, chances are it can be found here at Harold's.

But this is a restaurant and restaurants are about food and service. And visitors to Harold's are favored with both.

We arrive at the restaurant before 7 a.m. Five men are on stools at the counter. Others are at tables on a tile floor under a high ceiling, an indication on the age of the building.

Booths have red seats and black backs. The stools are red. After all red is Coca Cola's main color.

We are greeted by a male server. He is dressed in a black T-shirt that promotes the North Posey Vikings football team. A slogan on the back notes, "Excellence is not an act, but a habit." It is one, we suspect, the football team has heard time and again.

Sports bind small communities and Poseyville is no exception. Schedules for the North Posey athletic teams are on display near the cash register.

Our server, who has been at work since 4:30, is aided by another male and a woman, who also works the grill. She apologizes to us for a delay of the pancake order, saying she was unhappy with her first effort. Unsatisfactory servings are not passed on to the customer at Harold's. As the T-shirt says, excellence is not an act. It is a habit.

A feature of the breakfast menu is "Harold's B.E.L.T Sandwich." That's bacon, egg, lettuce and tomato, the price $1.95. Two hotcakes with bacon, ham or sausage are $3.40, French toast with sausage or bacon is $4.05. A western omelet with toast is $5.25, a full order of biscuits and gravy is $2.25.

Home style meals, "made from scratch," are among the restaurant's specials. Those homemade entrees, the desserts and the Coca Cola decor set Harold's apart from most restaurants in the area.

Patricia Wilson, the owner since the mid-1990s, identifies her clientele as farmers, factory workers, local families and travelers from Interstate 64, which can be exited at the interchange just north of Poseyville.

"I have the best regular customers a person could ask for. And the travelers who seek us out by driving into town are the most courteous and kind people you could ever meet," she adds.

Harold's is open from 4:30 a.m. to 2 p.m. Mondays through Saturdays and from 7 a.m. to 2 p.m. Sundays. Breakfasts and lunches draw about the same number of customers, but the early morning is the best time to observe the flavor of a small town. "That's when," the owner says, "men come in, sit around the 'table of wisdom' and talk about everything and everyone." And she asks, rhetorically, "But they do not gossip like women?"

It will be your loss if you drive on through the Posey County town without stopping at Harold's.

## NEW HARMONY

### THE MAIN CAFE

**526 North Main Street**

The Main Cafe isn't as old as the Harmony Society that George Rapp sought to establish here in the early 1800s. It has, however, been around for at least nine decades, a server tells us.

Like many small town diners, this one, too, is in an old two-story masonry building, one it shares with the Gallery shop in this tourist town.

Inside, the cafe is spotless with 20 seats at booths, 28 seats at tables. Green carpet matches the green and white table covers. But it is the walls and ceilings that set this diner apart from others. The walls are covered with hammered tin, the kind with patterns once seen in buildings dating back a century or more. The high ceiling is covered with the same type metal but of a different design.

A washboard that once made Monday laundry a backbreaking chore is on the wall as are historic pictures of the area.

It is just past 7 a.m. and the Main Cafe is quieter than it has been at times when we have stopped on earlier visits. A couple is at one table, a man is alone at a table for ten near the back. He greets another retiree with a silent nod, then continues to read the morning news. The new arrival orders a sausage sandwich and black tea, then begins to read another section of the paper. Little conversation is needed among friends.

They are soon joined by other men at what is obviously the community table where locals gather each morning.

Our waitress is pleasant, a woman past her youth, who enjoys her work and appreciates the community where she lives. She identifies the owner as Nina Duckworth and says the cafe is open from 5:30 a.m. to 1:30 p.m. Mondays through Saturdays.

The waitress helps make the cafe a different, more relaxing atmosphere than found at the fast food restaurants where teen-agers work for money rather than pleasure.

The cafe is the meeting place of New Harmony Kiwanians and the club's pennants, banners and citations are on one of the walls.

Anyone planning to spend a weekend in New Harmony should make it a point to dine at the New Harmony Cafe.

## BOONVILLE

### LOCUST STREET CAFE

**118 West Locust Street**

Locust Street is not Main Street. It is however eastbound Ind. 62, the westbound route on Main Street on the other side of the Warrick County Courthouse.

And it is the Courthouse workers and downtown employees that visitors are most likely to meet here in this old two-story yellow brick.

The 8 a.m. opening is too late for retirees who might otherwise congregate for coffee and conversation after feeding one of the meters out front. And the 2 p.m. closing is too early to bring in customers for evening meals.

The Locust Cafe is in a two-story building, a "Locust Street Cafe" sign on an awning over the sidewalk out front. "Open" says a sign board near the entrance which is faced with wood painted a beige color.

Step inside the green door and you'll find this is not your normal small town diner. This one is above average in decor, its menu a bit more varied. Owners Jan and Rick Tuley, owners since its opening in 1993, have seen to that.

There are numerous tables on carpet under low ceilings with fans. Sections are separated with wooden lattice dividers. The rough plywood walls are lined with an assortment of objects, old promotional calendars of Indiana University athletic teams, ice skates, baskets, musical instruments and outdated records, license plates, cameras. Think of an item and you may see it.

The furniture appears new, the place immaculate on this September Tuesday. It is 9:55 a.m. and most of the early arrivals have departed.

The pleasant aroma of a bakery is in the air, leading us to order a homemade cinnamon roll for $2. It is a meal in itself, fresh and tasty and, of course, cinnamony. It is homemade specialties like this that have made Locust Street a popular spot for diners tired of fast food lunches.

A menu feature this day is the "lite" lunch. It's a choice of grilled tenderloin, tuna salad or chicken salad, fruit or cottage cheese and low-fat muffin for $4.25. Swiss chicken with mashed potatoes and green beans is $4.35. A breaded tenderloin is $3.95, a cheeseburger $3.00, a turkey steak sandwich $4.35, a stuffed baked potato $2.75.

For a good breakfast or lunch remember to visit the Locust Street Cafe on a weekday. It's open from 8 a.m. to 2 p.m. Mondays through Fridays, but closed both Saturdays and Sundays.

# ROCKPORT

## MAIN STREET CAFE

### 105 Main Street

The Main Street Cafe is almost an oasis for diners. Except for snacks at convenience stores, it's one of the few restaurants on Ind. 66 between Newburgh and Tell City where motorists can sit down, sip coffee and enjoy a meal.

The cafe, owned by Carolyn Graham, is open from 5 a.m. to 2:30 p.m. (It may be open for evening meals in 2000).

Two blocks from the Spencer County Courthouse, the Main Street Cafe is in a two-story brick dating back to 1893, an engraving at the top notes. Windows face onto the sidewalk and a blue awning extends over the front door.

Inside there are only tables, no booths, no stools. Fans circulate quietly on the low ceiling. The dining room is neat, orderly with a sense of roominess not seen in some smaller, cramped diners elsewhere.

It still, however, has a small town flavor. Most of the customers know each other and are familiar with the waitresses. One man enters at mid-morning, walks behind a counter area, pours himself a cup of coffee and sits down, as casually as he would if he was at home.

Despite the lack of competition, prices are reasonable. A large order of biscuits and gravy is $2.75. Three pancakes with bacon are $2.99. A western omelet with ham, cheese, peppers, onions and tomatoes with potatoes on the side is $4.75.

We order eggs, basted, with toast. The waitress asks later about the eggs which are fried to perfection, without burned edges. She is pleased with our approval, explaining she has just started to use the grill.

Earlier in the morning, from 5 to 8, another woman, she says, has been both waitress and cook for the early arrivals. "It gets pretty hectic for her at times, " she adds.

A breakfast buffet is available from 5 a.m. to 11 a.m. on Saturdays, 6 a.m. to 10:30 a.m. on Sundays.

The lunch buffet changes daily. On this Monday it features corn bread and beans, wieners and kraut.

If the Main Street Diner had been in Rockport when Abe Lincoln was a teen, he might have stopped for breakfast before walking over the bluff and boarding his raft for New Orleans.

## DALE

### WINDELL'S CAFE

**6 West Medcalf**

**(Ind. 68 - just off Main Street)**

Windell's is more than a restaurant. It's a popular southern Indiana institution, one that boasts of family dining and catering since 1947.

Started by Bob and Margaret Windell, it has been owned by Darrel and Betty Jenkins since 1990. The Jenkins have maintained the same standards set by the Windells and the meals are still home cooked.

The result has been a loyal clientele. "The average age of our customers is 60 and up and a lot of them have eaten here 30 years or longer," the Jenkins agree. Seniors, it appears, like the good food, which includes daily specials, the wide selections of vegetables and, naturally, the 10 percent discount they are allowed.

This is a cafe that is not located in an ancient two-story brick. Windell's occupies its own building, a one-story structure that stands alone in the main part of town. A canopy over the sidewalk stretches across the entire front.

Windows face onto Ind. 68. Menus serve as place mats on the uncovered tables. Pictures line the walls. The decorations are seasonal, the choice for late September a Halloween motif.

Windell's is a big restaurant in a small town. About 110 seats are at booths and tables. Five seats are at one counter and ten more at what the owners call the "famed" horseshoe bar. That's bar as in soft drinks like coffee, milk and soda pop, not alcoholic beverages.

The restaurant is open from 6 a.m. to 8 p.m. daily, the only exceptions New Year's Eve, New Year's Day, Thanksgiving Day, Christmas Eve and Christmas.

Many area residents can be found at least once a day at Windell's. "It's the town's gathering place to discuss major topics (and, probably, some that aren't so major)," the Jenkins say. "Some regulars have to have the same seats two or three times a day."

The customers may tend to be older, but the servers and other helpers remain young. "Our employees are young people working their way through school and college. They normally stay four or five years, then face the real world having learned a lot about the public," the owners explain.

Windell's is near the intersection of Ind. 68 and U.S. 231, making it, the menu claims, "the eating place of Mid-America's crossroads."

Among the breakfast selections are two eggs with bacon or sausage, hash browns or German or American fries, with toast or biscuits for $4.00. Hotcakes with bacon or sausage is $3.50. A ham, cheese and mushroom omelet is $4.50, the same as the western omelet. Both come with toast. Biscuits and sausage gravy are $1.95.

As the noon hour approaches streams of diners begin arriving, knowing the food will be good whatever is on the menu. Specials are posted daily, today's being lasagna with garlic bread for $5.00.

Dinner entrees include roast beef and gravy, $5.75, and fried chicken, $5.75, white meat $6.00. Other items are shrimp, cod, chopped beef steak, liver and onions and pork chops. The salads and pies are on display in glass cases.

It isn't unusual for Windell's to serve 500 to 700 customers on weekends or up to 300 on weekdays.

Windell's obviously knows how to do things right. A restaurant doesn't stay in business for more than 50 years if it doesn't. Anyone near the I-64 and U.S. 231 ramps north of Dale, should drive down to Windell's. They can eat at a Denny's like the one at the interchange anytime.

## TELL CITY

### FREEZER CAFE
**626 Main Street**

It's appropriate that we end this book with a visit to one of Indiana's oldest Main Street diners.

If restaurants can be legends, the Freezer Cafe has become one in its 60 years as a fixture in this Ohio River city.

It appears to have changed little since it opened back in the 1930s. It still promises, the sign in the window notes, "good service, better prices, best food." Another announcement boasts that it is "the best little cafe around." And another claims it is "where friends meet."

Who is to argue with a business that has withstood floods and the arrival of fast food outlets, pizza parlors and trendy restaurants. The Freezer apparently has succeeded by being itself while changing little. Ownership doesn't change often, either, Karen Faucett having completed more than 18 years as the person in charge.

There is little upscale about the place, probably because its customers like it the way it is. It's in an unpretentious one-story building with a painting of a coffee cup on the side.

Inside, diners can sit at booths or tables or at one of the nine stools at the counter which faces a serving area. A small soda section is nearby, a remnant from the Freezer's origin as an ice cream shop. The front around the window is fashioned from six-inch square glass blocks, popular in an earlier era.

Selectors for juke box music are still on the wall at each booth. A radio, not a nickelodeon, however, is filling the diner with country music at mid-morning.

The breakfast menu offers a wide selection. The "Big Man" breakfast includes two eggs, two sausage links, two bacon strips, two hotcakes, hash browns and coffee for $3.95. The regular breakfast special features two eggs, ham, bacon or sausage, hash browns, a one-third order of biscuits and gravy, toast and coffee for $3.25.

For the cholesterol-minded, the "low-cal-high protein" breakfast includes one egg, a slice of toast and orange juice or coffee for $2.45.

The most expensive sandwiches served later are $2.50, which includes a rib-eye steak or the "Monster Burger."

The fare, says Karen Faucett, is "true old-fashioned home-cooking... the beans and potatoes kind. And the Freezer," she adds, "is still an attraction because it's one of the few remaining authentic old-fashioned cafes of an era that is almost gone."

"My pleasure," she says even after 18-plus years, "comes in brightening someone's day and having them leave with a smile." She recalls the time the cook put laughter into every customer's day: "She spilled a full pitcher of pancake mix. It covered one leg of her Navy pants from top to bottom. She lived too far away to go home and change and the longer her pants dried the stiffer they got. It had the customers in stitches, regardless what time they came in."

The Freezer Cafe is open from 4:30 a.m. to 7:30 p.m. Mondays through Thursdays and continuously... just like an old-time diner... from 4:30 a.m. Fridays to 7:30 p.m. Sundays.

As we leave we notice five cuckoo clocks on a wall near the front. They may be there just to prove that time has not passed the Freezer by, even after 60 years.

# INDEX


Akron . . . . . . . . . . . 83
Amboy . . . . . . . . . . 79
Atlanta . . . . . . . . . . 24
Bainbridge . . . . . . 163
Beech Grove . . . . . 11
Berne . . . . . . . . . . 120
Bicknell. . . . . . . . . 183
Bloomfield . . . . . . 169
Boonville. . . . . . . . 192
Boswell . . . . . . . . . 46
Brook . . . . . . . . . . . 52
Brooklyn . . . . . . . . . 15
Bookville. . . . . . . . 139
Brownstown . . . . . 151
Burlington . . . . . . . . 73
Butler . . . . . . . . . . 108
Camden . . . . . . . . . 76
Campbellsburg . . . 156
Carthage . . . . . . . 133
Cicero. . . . . . . . . . . 25
Clay City. . . . . . . . 166
Clayton . . . . . . . . . . 20
Cloverdale . . . . . . 164
Colfax. . . . . . . . . . . 69
Converse . . . . . . . . 78
Corydon . . . . . . . . 160
Culver. . . . . . . . . . . 89
Dale . . . . . . . . . . . 195
Delphi . . . . . . . . . . . 77
Dunkirk . . . . . . . . . 126
Edinburgh. . . . . . . . 13
Elwood . . . . . . . . . . 31
Etna Green. . . . . . . 92
Eugene. . . . . . . . . . 42
Fairmount . . . . . . . 115
Flora . . . . . . . . . . . 74
Fort Branch . . . . . 186
Fowler . . . . . . . . . . 47
Francesville . . . . . . 65
Franklin . . . . . . . . . 12
Freelandville. . . . . 182
Freemont . . . . . . . 107
Garrett . . . . . . . . . 100
Gas City . . . . . . . . 113
Gaston . . . . . . . . . 111
Geneva. . . . . . . . . 122
Goodland . . . . . . . . 49
Gosport . . . . . . . . 173
Greensburg . . . . . 137
Greens Fork . . . . . 130
Hartford City . . . . . 116
Hamlet . . . . . . . . . . 61
Hillsboro . . . . . . . . . 39
Howe . . . . . . . . . . 104
Jamestown . . . . . . . 22
Jasonville . . . . . . . 167
Jasper . . . . . . . . . 184
Jonesboro. . . . . . . 114
Kendallville . . . . . . 100
Kewanna . . . . . . . . 88
Knightstown . . . . . 131
Knox. . . . . . . . . . . . 62
Kouts . . . . . . . . . . . 59
Ladoga . . . . . . . . . . 35
Lagrange . . . . . . . 102
Laketon . . . . . . . . . 82
Lapel . . . . . . . . . . . 29
Leesburg . . . . . . . . 97
Liberty . . . . . . . . . 140
Linden . . . . . . . . . . 37
Linton . . . . . . . . . . 171
Lyons . . . . . . . . . . 176
Madison . . . . . . . . 144
Markle. . . . . . . . . . 119
Mechanicsburg. . . . 24
Mentone . . . . . . . . . 91
Mitchell . . . . . . . . . 152
Monon . . . . . . . . . . 48
Mooresville . . . . . . . 17
Morgantown . . . . . . 14
Morocco . . . . . . . . . 54
Nappanee. . . . . . . . 93
New Harmony . . . 191
New Paris. . . . . . . . 95
Noblesville . . . . . . . 27
North Judson . . . . . 63
North Salem . . . . . . 21
North Webster . . . . 96
Oakland City. . . . . 185
Odon . . . . . . . . . . 179
Orleans. . . . . . . . . 154
Owensville . . . . . . 188
Oxford . . . . . . . . . . 46
Parker City . . . . . . 128
Pennville. . . . . . . . 123
Perrysville. . . . . . . . 43
Pine Village . . . . . . 44
Plainfield. . . . . . . . . 18
Portland . . . . . . . . 124
Poseyville. . . . . . . 189
Remington . . . . . . . 54
Rensselaer. . . . . . . 56
Roann. . . . . . . . . . . 83
Rochester. . . . . . . . 86
Rockport. . . . . . . . 194
Rockville. . . . . . . . 165
Rome City . . . . . . 102
Rossville. . . . . . . . . 72
Rushville. . . . . . . . 135
Salem. . . . . . . . . . 157
Scotland . . . . . . . . 177
Shoals . . . . . . . . . 178
Spiceland . . . . . . . 131
Somerset . . . . . . . . 80
South Whitley . . . . . 99
St. Paul. . . . . . . . . 136
Stinesville . . . . . . . 149
Tell City. . . . . . . . . 197
Thorntown . . . . . . . 23
Tipton . . . . . . . . . . . 67
Van Buren. . . . . . . 117
Veedersburg . . . . . . 41
Vevay . . . . . . . . . . 143
Waldron . . . . . . . . . 32
Warren . . . . . . . . . 118
Waveland . . . . . . . . 36
Westfield . . . . . . . . 28
Westport. . . . . . . . 138
Wheatfield . . . . . . . 58
Winamac . . . . . . . . 64
Winchester . . . . . . 127
Wingate . . . . . . . . . 38
Woodburn. . . . . . . 109
Worthington . . . . . 174

# THE AUTHOR

*Main Street Diners* is author Wendell Trogdon's seventeenth book. A retired newspaper reporter and editor, his other titles include books about life in rural Indiana in the 1930s and 1940s, high school basketball and travel.

## NOSTALGIA BOOKS

*Those Were the Days*
*Through the Seasons*
*Carved in Memory*
*Back Home*
*The Country Bumpkin Gang*

## TRAVEL

*Backroads Indiana*
*Borderline Indiana*
*Indiana General Stores*
*U.S. 50—The Forgotten Highway*

## BIOGRAPHY

*Out Front: The Cladie Bailey Story*

## BASKETBALL

*No Harm No Foul: Referees Are People, Too*
*Basket Cases*
*Gym Rats: Sons Who Play For Fathers*
*Shooting Stars: Trek to a Championship*
*Whistle Blowers: A No Harm/No Foul Sequel*
*Damon—Living A Dream (co-authored with Damon Bailey)*

For more information about any of these books, contact the author at P. O. Box 651, Mooresville, IN 46158-0651, call him at 317-831-2815, or send an e-mail message to wend@iquest.net. You may order books from him or ask your favorite book store to obtain them.